Kingdom Progression

Insights into Kingdom Operation

Kingdom Progression

Insights into Kingdom Operation

Kristopher David Grepke

Kingdom Progression: Insights into Kingdom Operation
by Kristopher David Grepke

2023 All rights reserved.

Most Scripture quotations are from the ESV unless otherwise noted. Scriptures marked ESV are taken from the THE HOLY BIBLE, ENGLISH STANDARD VERSION (ESV): Scriptures taken from THE HOLY BIBLE, ENGLISH STANDARD VERSION ® Copyright© 2001 by Crossway, a publishing ministry of Good News Publishers.
Used by permission.

Scriptures marked KJV are taken from the KING JAMES VERSION (KJV): KING JAMES VERSION, public domain.

Scriptures marked NKJV are taken from the NEW KING JAMES VERSION (NKJV): Scripture taken from the NEW KING JAMES VERSION®. Copyright© 1982 by Thomas Nelson, Inc. Used by permission. All rights reserved.

"Scripture quotations taken from the (NASB®) New American Standard Bible®, Copyright © 1960, 1971, 1977, 1995, 2020 by The Lockman Foundation. Used by permission. All rights reserved. lockman.org"

Some Scriptures are from the New International Version®, NIV®. Copyright © 1973, 1978, 1984, 2011 by Biblica, Inc.™ Used by permission of Zondervan. All rights reserved worldwide. www.zondervan.com The "NIV" and "New International Version" are trademarks registered in the United States Patent and Trademark Office by Biblica, Inc.®

ISBN: 978-1-961482-04-3

Printed in the USA

Acknowledgments

I would be remiss if I did not express my appreciation and gratitude for those who partook in this journey with me. The result of this book would not be what it is without their treasured assistance.

I am grateful to Pastor Brian Lane and Pastor Brent Fisher for their wisdom and guidance in my life. They've known me at my worst and my best (so far). Not only have they provided me with wisdom and guidance, but they were also both instrumental in the completion of this book. Their insights into what has been written are greatly cherished.

I am likewise grateful for my father, Heath Grepke, who also read through what has been written and provided honest and constructive feedback. I am thankful to have such a good and strong godly influence as my father.

Additionally, I am thankful to Pastor Brent Fisher and Heath Grepke for being willing to honor me and this book by providing their honest thoughts that have been recorded in the Foreword section.

Of course, I could never forgive myself if I did not express my heartfelt love and appreciation for my wonderful wife, Audrey, who has never failed to encourage me while at the same time offering me truly constructive feedback.

Finally, this book and my ability to write such a thing would not even exist without the anointing of Jesus. I am eternally indebted to Him for all that He has done and continues to do in my life. May my life always point back to Him in all that I do.

Kristopher David Grepke

Table of Contents

~Foreword…7

~Introduction…9

~The Kingdom…13

~Can God Trust You?…35

~Ministry…67

~The Spiritual Gifts…101

~The Five-Fold Ministry…151

~The Call to All…185

~Epilogue…207

Foreword

In the day wherein we find ourselves, kingdoms of men are being reinvented and reimagined. It is imperative that we understand and align our lives with and in the Kingdom of Almighty God. To establish yourself in any kingdom, you must explore the purpose, nature, and the king of that kingdom. Only then can you discover the direction, the mannerisms, and the character of that kingdom. Being in harmonious melody with the heartbeat of the King creates the pulse of our "ministry." It is that circulatory rhythm that carries much-needed nutrients to the Body of Christ. When this alignment happens, an atmosphere of strength is created that is now able and willing to impact the next generation and build the Kingdom.

It has been a joy to see Kristopher grow into the godly man, author, and follower of Christ that he has become. His unique giftings have stretched his capacity for learning, and with a teaching spirit, he has already impacted many. Thank you to Kristopher for sharing these thoughts with your readers with the intent of furthering the Kingdom mindset.

I hope you enjoy these insightful words from the heart of a servant and allow them to impact your life. Allow this book to connect you to the rhythm of your ministry, so you too can be a thriving part of the Kingdom of God.

Pastor Brent Fisher

I do not consider myself to be an expert in many things. Not on ministry. Not on giftings. Honestly, I often feel I'm still learning. But I guess I might qualify as something of an expert on Kristopher Grepke.

I've been privileged to watch him grow from infancy to adulthood. From first steps to big steps. I've seen him make mistakes, and I've seen him avoid mistakes. And as he's matured, I've watched as he learned to pursue knowledge. His hunger to know and to understand has been tempered and cultivated in prayer and study and has allowed him to develop the heart of a teacher.

I count it a tremendous honor to introduce this author and this book.

I look forward to reading more of your work, of seeing more of your heart.

Forever proud,

Heath Grepke

Introduction

Greetings in the Name of Jesus, our Lord, and God.
Some time ago now I felt impressed by the Spirit to write to you all that has been written here. I pray, by the grace of God, I have written in a manner that is cohesive, and understandable. What has been written was not so merely because I could (even though my ability to write of these things comes by the grace of God alone), but because I felt a divine unction to do so. I feel that is important to stress at the outset. Just because we can do something, doesn't automatically mean we should. If we are sensitive and aware enough, He will lead us in every endeavor by His Word and Spirit.

Many books exist that pertain to the technicalities of ministry. I would not number what has been written here among such. Do not misunderstand, I'm not saying the technicalities shouldn't be focused on, because there is a time and place to do so. We need to understand the technicalities if we are to properly operate in every gift, calling, and anointing God has placed on us, and to a certain degree we will examine the technicalities; that is, however, not our focus. When speaking on the gifts, callings, and anointings of God the technicalities should never be our focus. Again, they are important to understand, but there are things of greater importance.

The title of this work has been in a state of flux for some time. The reason for this unsettled state is my desiring a title that would aptly convey the purpose and intent of what fills these pages. I give thanks to Pastor Brent Fisher for pointing me in the right direction. With his aid, the title "Kingdom Progression: Insights into Kingdom Operation" was cultivated. This, I feel, captures the essence of what Jesus has placed on my heart.

I fear that in pursuing ministry, many have a prioritized

mental understanding over relational experience. Never once do we read in Scripture of God placing mental understanding over a relationship. Many quote Hosea 4:6: "My people are destroyed for lack of knowledge." Yet they fail to understand that "knowledge" there refers to the understanding gained through intimate experience. Further, the Apostle Peter's last written words to the Church are an admonition to grow in grace first, then knowledge (see II Peter 3:18). Additionally, Jesus said that it would not be knowledge that demonstrates to people that we are His followers and ministers, but our love for others (see John 13:35). Finally, John declared that the way to measure how greatly one truly knows God is by examining their level of love toward others. For He is love, so to truly know Him is to abide in love (see I John 4:8). Therefore, the purpose of these things written is less to grow in mental understanding, and more to grow in relational understanding and experience.

    There are many who, in prayer, earnestly ask God to reveal their calling or reveal their purpose and ministry. I know this to be true because this was once a consistent prayer of mine. While this prayer request is by no means wrong, it fails to understand God's heart and how He works. God taught me that praying these kinds of prayers is not necessary if one is in the right relationship with Him. See, as we pursue Him in an intimate relationship, He will automatically unveil and reveal and pour out in our lives abundant blessings. The blessings ought to never become our motivation for seeking Him, or else our seeking Him is out of pride and not love. Yet, when we rightfully seek Him, He will reward us.

    Often when individuals think of the blessings of God, their minds gravitate toward those of a financial nature. Yet, His blessings far extend beyond this limited scope. For the gifts, callings, and anointings of God are a part of His blessings. Therefore, when we diligently seek Him in an intimate relationship, the fruit of that relationship will be the gifts, callings, and anointings that He has for us according to

His perfect will.

The author of Hebrews says it well when he says, "And without faith it is impossible to please him, for whoever would draw near to God must believe that he exists and that he rewards those who seek him" (Hebrews 11:6). He will reward when we seek.

Further, in terms of the reach of the things written here, I felt that it was meant to extend beyond a single group of people in the Church. The nature of this book is written progressively, each chapter leading into the next, while at the same time building upon the previous. Beginning with the foundation, we progress through to the various aspects of His Kingdom's operations. In this manner, this book acts as a roadmap to some. At the same time, each chapter can be read individually, not necessarily requiring the context of the previous chapter(s) (although the previous chapters may give additional insight, as they all connect at the end). In this manner, this book acts as a resource for others regarding the particular topic of which they are seeking understanding. I pray God has given me the grace to write accordingly.

It is my earnest prayer that this not just be another "good book" (assuming it is deemed "good"), but a genuine aid in the life of those diligently seeking to align themselves with Him and His Will. I pray He brings illumination and revelation, that your mind understands and your heart receives.

1
The Kingdom

The first thing of importance to understand is that God has a Kingdom. Jesus said that His Kingdom was not of this world (see John 18:36), "this world" was in reference to the natural realm. His Kingdom was not, nor is, like the earthly kingdoms. Rather, it is something supernatural. Neither is it what you might think it is. You might think of His Kingdom as Him sitting in Heaven with His angels. Such is not the case. In several places throughout the Gospels, Jesus speaks of the imminent arrival of His Kingdom (see Matthew 4:17 and Mark 1:15 as two examples). Then Jesus makes this statement: "For behold, the kingdom of God is in the midst of you" (Luke 17:21). The phrase translated "in the midst" is the Greek word "entos," which means "within; inside; or the inside." Therefore, rather than saying, "The Kingdom of God is in our midst," (which could be confusing, causing one to think that it is merely "around" them) we should instead say, "The Kingdom of God is within you, on the inside." This paints a much clearer picture of His Kingdom. However, all our questions pertaining to His Kingdom are not yet answered. For what does it mean for His Kingdom to be inside of us?

Speaking with Nicodemus, Jesus said this: "Truly, truly, I say to you, unless one is born again he cannot see the Kingdom of God" (John 3:3). There are two key things that we need to look at to fully understand this, that is "born again" and "see." Let's begin by looking at "see." The Greek word for "see" is "horaó," and it refers to several things, but all the different meanings of this word echo the same thing. "Horaó" refers to something that you experience, and to experience something is to partake of, or in, that thing. Therefore, unless you are born again you cannot partake of

God's Kingdom. Continuing with His instructions, Jesus utilizes the phrase, "born again." Nicodemus, obviously confused by this statement, prompts Jesus to further explain His instructions (see John 3:4). "Truly, truly, I say to you, unless someone is born of water and of the Spirit, he cannot enter the Kingdom of God" (John 3:5). To fully understand this, we must look to the words of Peter: "Repent, and each of you be baptized in the Name of Jesus Christ for the forgiveness of your sins; and you will receive the gift of the Holy Spirit" (Acts 2:38). It is vitally important that we understand all three of these crucial steps spoken by Peter, for neglecting even one causes all to be forsaken.

Repentance

First, we are called to repent. Repentance is the crucial first step, this is important, and it must come first. If sincere repentance does not come first, nothing else will follow. Without sincere repentance, baptism is just a bath. Without sincere repentance, God will not fill you with His Spirit. Sincere repentance must come first. What do I mean exactly by "sincere repentance?" Often when one thinks of repentance, this is what they think of: "I'm sorry." However, there is an old saying that goes, "Actions speak louder than words." Meaning, it is not so much what you say, but what you do. Breaking this down even more, it is not so much what you say or do, rather, it is the true motive and intent behind what you say and do. This is the idea behind repentance. That is why the psalmist said this: "For you will not delight in sacrifice, or I would give it; you will not be pleased with a burnt offering. The sacrifices of God are a broken spirit; a broken and contrite heart, O God, you will not despise" (Psalms 51:16-17). The words "broken" and "contrite" express very similar meanings in Hebrew. "Broken" is "shabar" meaning, "to break in pieces." Whereas "contrite" is "dakah" meaning, "to crush." One could surmise that

Kingdom Progression

David was painting this picture for us by combining these two words, describing one being so "broken in pieces" that they are completely and totally "crushed." Furthermore, we must look at this word "heart," for understanding this truly completes the understanding. "Heart" is "leb" in Hebrew. "Leb" is an amazing word: it holds such amazing weight. It means the "inner man, mind, will, and heart." David here is painting this picture for us (the picture being of himself after his affair) of one's entire being having been completely broken to the point of being crushed into dust. What does this mean? Is David saying that God wants us to be utterly broken? In a sense, yes. This is recorded in Chronicles: "If my people who are called by my name humble themselves, and pray and seek my face and turn from their wicked ways, then I will hear from Heaven and will forgive their sin and heal their land" (II Chronicles 7:14). I could be wrong, but I don't think there is a more clear understanding of repentance in all of Scripture than what is recorded here in II Chronicles. David recorded that what God desires is one who truly comes to Him broken and crushed, not one coming to Him out of religious duty. II Chronicles records the same. God will only "hear from Heaven...forgive their sins and heal their land" after they have, one, humbled themselves, and, two, turned from their wicked ways. "Humble" is "kana" and it means, "to bring one's self into subjection." This, then, is true, sincere repentance: coming to God truly broken and crushed over your wickedness, fully willing to surrender your sinful self to Him for Him to come and take over, and then truly turning away from that thing you were so broken over. If you "repented" but then went right back to that same sin, you did not repent. Rather, you fulfilled a religious duty, and it is such things that God "does not delight in" and "takes no pleasure in."

It is important to note that after sincere repentance has taken place, there is no specific order in which things must occur. One could be baptized after sincere repentance and then receive His Spirit. However, one could also receive His Spirit after sincere repentance and then be baptized (compare Acts 10:44-48 to Acts 19:1-6). The crucial part is sincere repentance coming first. One knows that they have offered unto God sincere repentance based on His response. What is God's response to sincere repentance? "And fire came out from before the LORD and consumed the burnt offering and the pieces of fat on the altar, and when all the people saw it, they shouted and fell on their faces" (Leviticus 9:24). God consumes the sincere sacrifice (repentance) with fire. What is the Holy Spirit equated to in the New Testament? Fire (see Matthew 3:11; Luke 3:16).

Baptism

Continuing with Peter's flow in Acts 2:38, let's continue with baptism. The "why" and "how" of baptism are widely misunderstood, so my aim here is to present a simple understating of baptism in water to bring about a clear and concrete understanding.

Numerous different Christian denominations proclaim baptism to simply be a "confession of faith," but such an idea is never presented in Scripture. The Bible is very clear as to the "why" of baptism. If we look back to our text (Acts 2:38), Peter linked the baptism of water with the "forgiveness of sins." "Forgiveness" is "aphesis" in Greek, it means, "releasing someone from obligation or debt; pardon; complete forgiveness." Baptism, when preceded by sincere repentance (as talked about previously), removes all sin from the one baptized (see also II Corinthians 5:17). Expounding upon the "why," Paul tells us, "For as many of you as were baptized into Christ have put on Christ" (Galatians 3:27 NKJV). Being "baptized into Christ" refers to the "how" of baptism (which we will come back to here shortly). After we complete the "into" we reach the "put on." These two words are one word in Greek, "enduo." "Enduo" means

Kingdom Progression

"being clothed with." Therefore, when we are "baptized into Christ," we then become engrafted into Him. Further, we become engrafted into His Name. Think of it like a family. Apart from Christ, we are orphans. This is why Jesus proclaimed, "I will not leave you as orphans; I will come to you" (John 14:18). We are alone and separated from our Father, but He sought to restore that divide, that separation. All three steps of salvation laid out in Acts 2:38 are integral to this, each playing a different key part. The part baptism plays is, one, cleansing us of unrighteousness and sin and, two, placing His family Name on us. This is essential, for if we are not a part of His family, how can we dwell in His home? We must become His adopted sons and daughters to partake of His dwelling. There is more to this which we will get into with receiving His Spirit.

It is of vital importance to understand what baptism looks like, and this plays into the "how" part. The word "baptize" (as in Acts 2:38) is "baptizō" which means, "to immerse; to submerge; to make fully wet." Throughout the different Christian denominations, there are several different modes of baptism practiced, such as sprinkling or splashing, partial submersion, and full submersion. However, if we dig into the original language of the text, we see that full immersion is the proper mode of baptism. This is fully understood when one understands that baptism in water is us taking part in His burial. The old man is buried, and the new man comes out of the water. We will talk more about this at the conclusion of this chapter.

Before we can dive into that, we must further understand the "how" of baptism. There is a proper "how." If we look back, once again, to Acts 2:38 we see Peter proclaim that baptism must take place "in the name of Jesus." However, if we look at Matthew 28:19, Jesus declares for all to be baptized in the Name of the Father, Son, and Holy Spirit. What is this? Is the Bible contradicting itself? Was Peter rebelling against the teachings of Jesus? Certainly not!

Kristopher David Grepke

We must understand how Jesus taught. Jesus' primary mode of teaching was parables, metaphors, and riddles. Why? Why did He not simply say it plainly? Because Jesus was inviting relationships (see Matthew 13:10-15). While Jesus does not wish death on anyone (see II Peter 3:9), He also does not want just anyone following Him. What do I mean by that? He wants those who truly love Him and are truly devoted to Him. He desires love, not mere religious tradition (in the sense of man's traditions). Therefore, He spoke and taught in a way that would force whoever was listening to truly dig out the meaning of what He said. The only people that would put forth the effort to dig into His teachings were those who truly desired Him. He didn't make it impossible to understand Him, for to anyone willing to put forth a little effort, His teachings can be fully understood. He left us many clear "clues" as to what He was trying to convey. One such "clue," in Matthew 28:19, is the use of the singular word "name." He tells us three seemingly names (Father, Son, Holy Spirit) but then proclaims a singular Name. What this tells us is that these three are titles, not names. These three titles are attributed to one Name. This singular Name is Jesus (see John 5:43; John 14:26; John 20:31). We know, then, that Peter had it right when he declared, "In the name of Jesus." Again, the "why" is washing away of sin and being engrafted into His family, and the "how" is in His Name, Jesus. Baptism in Jesus' Name is the pattern we see repeated throughout the Book of Acts (see Acts 2:38; 8:12,35-38; 10:47-48; 19:1-6; 22:16). Not once in all of Scripture do we see anyone baptized in the titles. There is no power in titles, only in the Name.

The essentiality of baptism cannot be over-stressed. Jesus gives us a parable that expresses its cruciality. Matthew 22:1-14 records said parable regarding His return. It begins with Him sending out His representatives to invite guests of high stature, but they all made excuses for why they couldn't attend. He then admonishes His representatives to take the invitations to the streets and invite all, with the stipulation that they must wear His provided wedding garments. This is where we see this interaction: "But when the king came in to look at the guests, he saw there a man who had no wedding garment. And he said to him, 'Friend, how did you get in here without a wedding garment?' And he was speechless. Then the king said to the attendants, 'Bind him hand and foot and cast him into the outer darkness. In that place there will be weeping and gnashing of teeth'" (Matthew 22:11-13). This parable provides key insight, for it is describing one who was caught up in the Rapture at the End. Meaning, this individual had received His Spirit. He was made alive. However, the individual overlooked the cruciality of baptism in His Name. As we discussed previously, when we are baptized into Christ we put on Christ. Baptized into His Name, we take on Him. These were the wedding garments the man forsook to put on. What we see is that one can be made alive by His Spirit and be caught up at the End, but if they have not put on Christ, they will not be permitted to stay with His family.

Infilling of His Spirit

Now we come to receiving His Spirit. This, too, has a "why" and not a "how," rather, a sign, a confirmation. First, as with baptism, we must understand the "why." To properly understand the "why," we must go back to the beginning.

Man was created as a spiritual being housed in a physical vessel (see Genesis 2:7). This spiritual being was directly connected to God's Spirit, as it was His Spirit breathed into us that gave us life. However, He cannot dwell where there is sin. As the Prophet Isaiah said, "But your iniquities have made a separation between you and your God, and your sins have hidden his face from you so that he does not hear" (Isaiah 59:2). It is also vitally important to understand that God gave Adam and Eve a choice in the

Garden of Eden because true love is a choice (see Genesis 2:16-17). This choice was between unity and a relationship with Him, or the lustful desires of self. The key thing here is God warning them that if they pursued the desires of self, the sinful desires, they would die. As Paul wrote, "For the wages of sin is death…" (Romans 6:23a). Interestingly, if we go to the next chapter in Genesis when Adam and Eve partook of sin, they did not drop dead. God proclaimed they would! What then is this? Did God lie? Not at all. On that day Adam and Eve did die, just not physically. They died spiritually. The unity with God they were created in, and the relationship they had with Him, died the moment they disobeyed and partook of sin. Now there was only a divide. To put it quite literally, man had become a husk of their former self. This is not what God desired. He did not create humanity simply to watch them from afar, He created humanity to have someone to love and to have someone to love Him. What we see next is God giving a prophetic promise of redemption: "I will put enmity between you and the woman, and between your offspring and her offspring; He shall crush your head, and you shall bruise His heel" (Genesis 3:15). This did not come to pass immediately, even still, the price for sin had to be paid. However, man could not do this, for something to be worthy of atoning for sin, it had to be spotless and perfect, and man was flawed and sinful. God then instituted animal sacrifices to atone for sin (see Exodus 29:10-14 as one example). Herein lies the issue: animals cannot perfectly cover the sin of humanity for animals are inferior to humans. Humanity was created in the image of God, animals were not (see Hebrews 10:4-10). God knew for the sin of humanity to be covered completely, a perfect human would have to die, but He also knew that no human could ever do this. He, therefore, declared that He would be the perfect sacrifice and atone for our sin by dying a death He didn't deserve. As the author of Hebrews puts it, "He entered once for all into the holy places, not by means of the blood of goats and calves

Kingdom Progression

but by means of His own blood, thus securing an eternal redemption" (Hebrews 9:12). Also, John said, "He is the propitiation for our sins, and not for ours only but also for the sins of the whole world" (I John 2:2). "Propitiation" is "hilasmos" in Greek, meaning "atoning sacrifice." Now that God had eternally paid the price of sin, the divide could be mended. Unity and relationship, restored. Now He could fulfill the numerous prophecies He had spoken through His Old Testament Prophets pertaining to the pouring out of His Spirit (see Ezekiel 36:26-27 and Joel 2:28-29 as two examples). It is only when we receive His Spirit that unity is restored and we receive power over the sin that once had us bound. If we do not receive His Spirit, there is still no unity, and we are still bound by sin.

Paul put it best when he wrote, "Or do you not know that the unrighteous will not inherit the kingdom of God? Do not be deceived: neither the sexually immoral, nor idolaters, nor adulterers, nor men who practice homosexuality, nor thieves, nor the greedy, nor drunkards, nor revilers, nor swindlers will inherit the kingdom of God. And such were some of you. But you were washed, you were sanctified, you were justified in the name of the Lord Jesus Christ and by the Spirit of our God" (I Corinthians 6:9-11). He said another thing, much to the same effect, in Titus, "But when the goodness and loving kindness of God our Savior appeared, he saved us, not because of works done by us in righteousness, but according to his own mercy, by the washing of regeneration and renewal of the Holy Spirit, whom he poured out on us richly through Jesus Christ our Savior, so that being justified by his grace we might become heirs according to the hope of eternal life" (Titus 3:4-7). Jesus, Himself said, "It is the Spirit who gives life..." (John 6:63a). Without receiving His Spirit, one, we are still dead, and, two, we have no place in His Kingdom.

Going back to baptism, I mentioned how being baptized in His Name puts His Name on us, it declares that we are adopted sons and daughters. However, baptism without receiving His Spirit is pointless. Being baptized and having His Name spoken over you, but never receiving His Spirit simply means that you should have gone home, but didn't.

As I said previously, along with a "why" for His Spirit, there is also a sign. Some may ask why God gives a distinct sign to accompany the infilling of His Spirit. Speaking on the nature of God, Paul said this: "For God is not a God of confusion (disorder), but of peace" (I Corinthians 14:33). One of the fundamental aspects of who God is, is that He is a God of order, not chaos. If there was no obvious, immediate, and evident sign then all there would be is confusion, or chaos. He gives signs to ensure order, remove doubt, and build faith (we will look at this aspect of His nature a little further later on). In addition to this, looking to the Old Testament, every time God instituted a new covenant with an individual, there was a visible sign that accompanied such. For example, the covenant God made with Abraham was instituted with circumcision (see Genesis 17:9-13). God continues this pattern of pairing covenants with signs in the New Testament.

Looking to the Book of Acts, at the outset of chapter two this sign is revealed to us: "When the day of Pentecost arrived, they were all together in one place. And suddenly there came from heaven a sound like a mighty rushing wind, and it filled the entire house where they were sitting. And divided tongues as of fire appeared to them and rested on each one of them. And they were all filled with the Holy Spirit and began to speak in other tongues as the Spirit gave them utterance" (Acts 2:1-4). Throughout Scripture (both the Old Testament and the New Testament) it is stated that for something to be given heed to, there must be two or three witnesses (see Deuteronomy 17:6; 19:15; John 8:17; and II Corinthians 13:1 as a few examples). This is how we must interpret Scripture. When examining a particular passage

Kingdom Progression

that seems to convey a particular truth, we must examine Scripture to see if there are two or three witnesses that can attest to it. We take that understanding and apply it to these verses here in Acts 2. Upon examining this passage in correlation to the rest of the Book of Acts in particular, we find that there is a common sign that is documented. In every case in which an individual (or individuals) was filled with His Spirit, they spoke in other tongues (here in Acts 2:1-4; Acts 10:44-48; Acts 19:1-6 along with several others that allude to the same experience such as Acts 8). We know then that this sign, speaking with other tongues, is the sign given to us that we would know when we have received His Spirit. Without the sign being manifested, there has been no infilling.

Some may, and indeed some have, ask the question, why speaking in tongues? At the end of the day, He is sovereign and can make whatever choices He desires for His creation. Therefore, to a degree, all we can say is that it is His sovereign will for speaking in other tongues to be the sign. However, because He desires to be known by us, He has left us clues that point to His thought behind this sign.

First, looking to Genesis 11:1-9 we read the account of the Tower of Babel. Man was unified in one tongue. Their unity gave them great strength to be able to accomplish great things. However, their hearts were set on evil only, so their unity of tongue was used to glorify man and not God. To do away with this unified evil, God came down and "confused the language of the whole word" (v.9). Thereby, the dividing of tongues brought disunity. Fast forward to the Book of Acts, we now see God perform a divine reversal, for He desired there to be unity now, not disunity. Therefore, He brought the people of His Kingdom back together, unified in one tongue.

The second insight we are given comes from James 3:1-8. In this passage the Apostle James talks about the power of the tongue, specifically, he talks about how the tongue cannot be tamed by any man (v.8). He states that even the most unruly beasts of the field can be tamed by man, but not their own tongues (v.7). Therefore, when the individual surrenders to God and allows Him to fill them with His Spirit, He takes control of the most unruly member of the whole body. The sign of speaking in tongues is evidence that the individual has completely surrendered to Him, for He has control of even the most stubborn and uncontrollable member.

Pursuing His Kingdom

However, we cannot stop here. These three key aspects birth you into the Kingdom of God, which is why it is referred to as the New Birth, but one must remain in the Kingdom of God. We cannot accept the philosophy of "once saved, always saved," for such a mentality is unbiblical. Salvation is not just a moment, it is also a pursuit. One is not truly saved until they pass through into Heaven. As long as we remain in this life, on this sinful earth, we must pursue salvation. What does this mean?

At several points throughout the Gospels, Jesus conveys to us that we must take up our cross in order to follow Him. However, there is one particular passage I feel conveys it the best: "And he said to all, 'If anyone would come after me, let him deny himself and take up his cross daily and follow me'" (Luke 9:23). James said this, much to the same effect: "Submit yourselves therefore to God. Resist the devil, and he will flee from you. Draw near to God, and he will draw near to you. Cleanse your hands, you sinners, and purify your hearts, you double-minded...Humble yourselves before the Lord, and he will exalt you" (James 4:7-8, 10). Both of these passages of Scripture echo the same truth; we are called to daily (as Jesus proclaimed) submit to and pursue God but also to daily repent of our wickedness and allow Him to purify us. As John proclaimed, "If we

Kingdom Progression

confess our sins to him, he is faithful and just to forgive us our sins and to cleanse us from all unrighteousness" (I John 1:9). Faithfully and sincerely doing these things is an act of humility, and if we humble ourselves before Him, He will lift us.

We also must understand that speaking in tongues is not a one-time thing. Paul said, "I thank God that I speak in tongues more than all of you" (I Corinthians 14:18), indicating that he did so often. Paul understood that praying in tongues was not just some show, but it had deep, spiritual implications. He stated, "Likewise the Spirit helps us in our weakness. For we do not know what to pray for as we ought, but the Spirit himself intercedes for us with groaning too deep for words" (Romans 8:26). Jude declared: "But you, beloved, building yourselves up in your most holy faith and praying in the Holy Spirit" (Jude 1:20). Praying (speaking) in tongues is not only Him praying through us when we don't know what or how to pray, but it also builds us up and strengthens our faith. It helps us with our weaknesses. These are just two examples of what the Spirit does in the life of one who is faithful in prayer. There is so much more. The point here is, we are called to pursue Him intentionally and with full devotion. We are called to humble ourselves before Him in sincere repentance, daily. And when we pursue Him sincerely, He draws near to us, and we are consumed by His Spirit.

Not long ago (from the time of writing this) a man of God that I greatly look up to, preached a deeply convicting message on the cup that Jesus agonized over in the Garden. He talked about how we want the things of God, we want to be used, we want to go deeper, and we want this and that. However, God has placed a cup before us, and we will never reach those things until we drink the cup. Thinking about this, my mind went to the Gospel of Matthew. The mother of James and John came to Jesus and said how she wanted them to be positioned on the right and left of Him in His Kingdom.

Jesus' response was this: "You do not know what you are asking. Are you able to drink the cup that I am about to drink?" (Matthew 20:22). What is the cup? What was Jesus agonizing over? Jesus said this when praying about the cup: "Yet not as I will, but as you will" (Matthew 26:39). The cup is total submission to God. The cup is a life of complete, sincere devotion. The cup cannot be looked over if one is to do all that God has called them to.

Holiness

We cannot speak on pursuing His Kingdom or subjecting our will to His without speaking on holiness. As the author of Hebrews stated, "Strive for peace with everyone, and for the holiness without which no one will see the Lord" (Hebrews 12:14). There are several key aspects that bear examination from this Scripture.

"Strive" here is "dioko" which means, "to run swiftly in order to catch a person or thing; to pursue; to chase after." What we see at the start is that holiness is not something achieved through idleness, but something sought after with intentionality. One definition of "dioko" describes it as a hostile pursuit, implying the tenacity in which one pursues the thing sought after. "Holiness" is "hagiasmos" which means just that, "holiness or sanctification." This word also means, "the process in which the believer is transformed by the Lord into His likeness." The word "see" is one looked at previously from John 3:5, it refers to actually experiencing a thing. Therefore, what we see is that if one is not intentionally, actively, and almost aggressively pursuing the grace of God in their lives that transforms them into His image, they cannot experience Him, which would include His Kingdom.

Holiness is multifaceted. When many hear "holiness" their minds go to outward appearance. While this is a major aspect of holiness, it is not the most important. The most important aspect of holiness is the inward manifestation thereof. The inward aspect of holiness is the most crucial, for it is the catalyst to outward holiness.

Proverbs 23:7 states, "As a man thinks in his heart, so is he." "Thinks" is "sha'ar" and it paints a very clear picture. It refers to one who guards a gate to judge what is allowed in and out. The word "heart" is "nephesh" which is a very interesting word. It can refer to a multitude of things encompassing both the inward aspect of an individual (the mind, desires, and will) and the outward aspect (the manifestation of such things). By Solomon using such wording he was conveying that what we allow into our inward man is then sent to be displayed outwardly. We very clearly see then that the inward affects the outward, for Solomon declared, "So is he."

Beyond this though, the outward manifestation without the inward being present, is hypocrisy. It is a show for man, not for God. God cares more about the inward, as He declared in I Samuel 16:7, but this is not to say that the outward does not matter. For as stated, the outward is a direct result of the inward. When the inward is right, the outward will automatically follow. However, we cannot mix up the order of these, attempting to place the outward without the inward first. As Jesus stated, quoting Isaiah 29:13, "You hypocrites! Well did Isaiah prophesy of you, when he said: 'This people honors me with their lips, but their heart is far from me; in vain do they worship me, teaching as doctrines the commandments of men'" (Matthew 15:7-9).

Some attempt to argue holiness, claiming that it is man attempting to save themselves. They quote Ephesians 2:8-9 which proclaims that we are not saved by works but by His grace and faith in such. What they neglect is the very next verse, "For we are his workmanship, created in Christ Jesus for good works, which God prepared beforehand, that we should walk in them" (Ephesians 2:10). We were created in Christ Jesus, which refers to the new creation that is born through the New Birth, for good works. What Paul is saying through these three verses is, we are saved by faith in His grace and after one is saved (experiencing the New Birth) we walk in that New Birth through good works. This may still sound like we are doing the work, but such is still not the case. Paul stated, "For it is God who works in you, both to will and to work for his good pleasure" (Philippians 2:13). This is what is seen: after receiving His Spirit at the New Birth, He then begins to work in the individual to give them both the desire and the ability to walk in His holiness, which pleases Him. It is still by His grace that we walk in pursuit of holiness. Without His grace, we would have no concept of holiness or the slightest ability to attain it.

This is not to say that we can just then sit back and do nothing and simply watch as He does everything. Such an idea would imply that we are mindless beings with no will. This is not the case, for when God created humanity in the Garden of Eden, He gave them a choice between Him and self-glorification (see Genesis 2:15-17, 3:1-7). Man had to decide for himself whom he would serve. Moses issued this statement to the people in the wilderness: "I call heaven and earth to witness against you today, that I have set before you life and death, blessing and curse. Therefore choose life, that you and your offspring may live, loving the LORD your God, obeying his voice and holding fast to him, for he is your life and length of days, that you may dwell in the land that the LORD swore to your fathers, to Abraham, to Isaac, and to Jacob, to give them" (Deuteronomy 30:19-20). Not just the blessings and fulfillment of His promises were contingent on their obedience and submission, but also their very life.

Bringing this to our day, when Jesus died on the cross for the sins of humanity, all were not automatically saved. There was an active choice that had to be made on the part of the individual as to whether or not they were going to submit their will to His Will. This is not limited

Kingdom Progression

to the New Birth, for even after initial salvation we must actively submit to Him to allow His grace to work in us. If this were not the case and all were automatically saved and sanctified, why would Peter have stated that "The Lord is not slow to fulfill his promise as some count slowness, but is patient toward you, not wishing that any should perish, but that all should reach repentance" (II Peter 3:9) Jesus, Himself said, "Not everyone who says to me, 'Lord, Lord,' will enter the kingdom of heaven, but the one who does the will of my Father who is in heaven" (Matthew 7:21). Truly experiencing His Kingdom requires much more than simply stating that He is Lord. It requires allowing His Will to have preeminence which requires us to forsake our will.

Back to holiness, as stated, true holiness begins inwardly. This means allowing the character of God to be developed in you. Paul conveys what this looks like: "But the fruit of the Spirit is love, joy, peace, patience, kindness, goodness, faithfulness, gentleness, self-control; against such things there is no law. And those who belong to Christ Jesus have crucified the flesh with its passions and desires" (Galatians 5:22-24). These nine attributes sum up the totality of God's nature. All that He is and does falls into one, or multiple, of these nine characteristics. When we allow the transforming power of God (His grace) to work in us, what Paul conveys here will be the result. The key to fully understanding this is given in the preceding verses. Before this Paul lists the works, or fruit, of the flesh. He ends that list with, "and things like these" (v.21). However, no such modifier is placed alongside the Fruit of the Spirit. Meaning, if one is not operating in the Fruit of the Spirit, they are, therefore, operating in the fruit of the flesh.

When one truly operates in the Fruit of the Spirit, outward holiness will follow. Paul admonished us, "I appeal to you therefore, brothers, by the mercies of God, to present your bodies as a living sacrifice, holy and acceptable to God, which is your spiritual worship. Do not be conformed to this world, but be transformed by the renewal of your mind, that by testing you may discern what is the will of God, what is good and acceptable and perfect" (Romans 12:1-2). Paul here is talking about our physical bodies, our outward appearance. He admonishes us to present such as a "living sacrifice," and not to allow our physical bodies to be "conformed to this world." The phrase "living sacrifice" refers to something devoted to another. A sacrifice was brought unto the temple to be devoted as a sacrifice unto the Lord. In the same fashion, we are to present ourselves. This sacrifice, this "spiritual worship," is a dying to oneself through selfless devotion. It is a call to step outside of what is normal, comfortable, and easy. To sacrifice means to give up something that is desired. It is not throwing away something that is not cared about, but something that matters to the individual. We do this by not being "conformed to this world." "Conformed" is "syschēmatizō" and it means, "to conform to the same pattern." What is the pattern to which we are not to conform? The world's. Meaning, we are called to stand out from the world. We are to not look like the world. We are to not do what the rest of the world does. As Peter stated, "But ye are a chosen generation, a royal priesthood, an holy nation, a peculiar people; that ye should shew forth the praises of him who hath called you out of darkness into his marvellous light" (I Peter 2:9 KJV). The word "peculiar" is "peripoiēsis" and it means a "peculiar possession." The word "peculiar" means something unique to someone. For example, every writer has a "peculiar," or unique style. The fact we are called to be His "peculiar possession" means that we are to be unique. Meaning, if we look, act, and talk like the rest of the world, we need to evaluate if we have truly become His possession.

There are a few ways in which we display outward holiness. First, our speech. Paul stated, "Let no corrupting talk come out of your mouths, but only such as is good for building up, as fits the occasion, that it may give grace to those who hear" (Ephesians 4:29). He also stated, "But now you must put them all away: anger, wrath, malice, slander, and obscene talk from your mouth. Do not lie to one another, seeing that you have put off the old self with its practices and have put on the new self, which is being renewed in knowledge after the image of its creator" (Colossians 3:8-10).

Next, our actions. Paul strongly conveyed, "Look carefully then how you walk, not as unwise but as wise, making the best use of the time, because the days are evil. Therefore do not be foolish, but understand what the will of the Lord is. And do not get drunk with wine, for that is debauchery, but be filled with the Spirit, addressing one another in psalms and hymns and spiritual songs, singing and making melody to the Lord with your heart, giving thanks always and for everything to God the Father in the name of our Lord Jesus Christ, submitting to one another out of reverence for Christ" (Ephesians 5:15-21). Peter echoed this more simply, "But as he who called you is holy, you also be holy in all your conduct, since it is written, 'You shall be holy, for I am holy'" (I Peter 1:15-16). "Conduct" is "anastrophē" and it means, "all manner of life; conduct; behavior." It encompasses every aspect of outward living.

Third, our presentation. Our apparel. What we put on. Moses stated, "A woman shall not wear a man's garment, nor shall a man put on a woman's cloak, for whoever does these things is an abomination to the LORD your God" (Deuteronomy 22:5). Paul also stated, "I desire then that in every place the men should pray, lifting holy hands without anger or quarreling; likewise also that women should adorn themselves in respectable apparel, with modesty and self-control, not with braided hair and gold or pearls or costly attire, but with what is proper for women who profess godliness—with good works" (I Timothy 2:8-10). Peter agreed, "Do not let your adorning be external—the braiding of hair and the putting on of gold jewelry, or the clothing you wear— but let your adorning be the hidden person of the heart with the imperishable beauty of a gentle and quiet spirit, which in God's sight is very precious" (I Peter 3:3-4). What we see, without deep study, is that there should be a distinction between the sexes. Along with that distinction, there should be modesty and self-control and nothing that glorifies the self. All that we do should bring glory to God.

Another aspect of our presentation is makeup and jewelry. Every time the Bible mentions a woman wearing makeup it is mentioned in a negative connotation. One such example is II Kings 9:30-37 where Jezebel attempted to seduce Jehu by "painting her face." Another example is in Proverbs chapters 5-7, Solomon gives several warnings against adulterous women. One key detail about such women is that they seduce with their "eyelashes." This word can also be translated as "eyelid" which implies that their eyelids and lashes are painted to entice. We see that makeup's primary purpose is seduction. Even if this isn't the active motivation of one who wears such, it is the underlying purpose behind it, nonetheless. Furthermore, there is much that can be said about jewelry, but to summarize why jewelry is wrong is to look back at I Timothy 2:8-10 and I Peter 3:3-4. We are called to not adorn ourselves, to not glorify the flesh. We are called to not draw attention to us but to Him. By wearing jewelry, we do just what we ought not to do, draw attention to ourselves.

One final area is hair. In I Corinthians 11:2-16, Paul gives vital teaching on the proper distinction between men and women in a proper relationship with God. Paul states that when approaching God in prayer or seeking to be used in prophecy (which could be any form of anointed speaking), the man's head ought to be uncovered and the woman's covered. Paul then clarifies that the covering he is speaking of is hair (v.14-15). He states that for men to have long hair it is a shame, but for a woman to have such it is her glory. "Long hair" is "komaō" which refers to uncut hair. For men

Kingdom Progression

to have uncut hair is a "disgrace," "atimia," which is also "vile." Meaning, it is an abomination unto God. However, for women, it is her "glory." This is "doxa." This word refers to many things, but one such thing is beautiful in the eyes of God or belonging unto God. Meaning, when a woman has uncut hair, God sees her as His own.

Conclusion

Why have I spent the first portion of this book talking about the Kingdom of God? It is simple if you think about it. If one is to understand their gifting, one must first understand that God has a Kingdom, and it is His Kingdom that they are called to. However, we cannot speak of His Kingdom without understanding how one enters His Kingdom. Furthermore, we cannot simply speak about one entering His Kingdom, we must also understand what one must do to abide in His Kingdom. Drink the cup. For to look over any of these things would be an injustice and disservice. For we do not serve our own kingdom, nor does His Kingdom abide by our standard. We abide by His standard.

When speaking on baptism, I briefly mentioned how when one is baptized of water, it is them partaking in His burial. It is important to understand that His passion (His death, burial, and resurrection) laid the groundwork, or the foundation, for our new life in Him, or the New Birth. Just as He died, so we too must die to ourselves in repentance. We must humble ourselves and submit our will and desires unto Him so that His Will and desires become manifested within us (see Luke 9:23). However, we cannot stop there. For He was also buried, therefore we, too, must be buried. We are buried with Him in baptism in His Name. The old man goes down in the water, and the new man springs forth (see II Corinthians 5:17). Finally, we must also understand that Jesus did not stay in the grave but rose in victory. We too are called to walk in victory, however, this is only possible by His Spirit. For we cannot save ourselves from sin, it was only His perfect sacrifice that could do such. By Him giving us His Spirit, He bestows upon us that same overcoming power (see Ephesians 2:4-6).

It is truly of vital importance that we understand the New Birth, for such lays the foundation for all other aspects of His Kingdom. I understand many will read this that experienced the New Birth long ago, but there are still those struggling to fully understand what happened to them, and before they can truly understand the deeper things, they must understand these fundamental truths. I hope that what has been written here has aided in the growth of understanding.

I feel it important to emphatically state that we are not discussing salvation by works. Paul said we are saved by grace through faith, it is not of any man (see Ephesians 2:8-9). Repentance is not a work, it is a sincere surrender of ourselves to God. Baptism is not a work, it is humble obedience to His Word where we take on His Name and are washed clean of our sinful nature (see I Peter 3:21). Further, receiving His Spirit is not a work, it again requires a heart of surrender. One yields to God, and only once there has been a surrender does He take control.

In regards to living a life of holiness, many have tried to protest that this falls under salvation by works and they quote Ephesians 2:8-9 as a testament. But they forsake the very next verse, "For we are his workmanship, created in Christ Jesus for good works, which God prepared beforehand, that we should walk in them" (Ephesians 2:10). Having been saved by His grace through faith, He then gives us the power to walk in a manner which is pleasing unto Him, or, good works, or holiness.

Kingdom Progression

2
Can God Trust You?

In the previous chapter, we conveyed that God has a Kingdom. We explored how entrance into His Kingdom is through the New Birth. However, one must also intentionally and continually pursue Him to retain citizenship. Those who are saved and who do pursue, as I said, are the citizens or the people of His Kingdom. Every kingdom has a people or it is not a kingdom. Furthermore, every kingdom has a king. Jesus is our King (see Revelation 19:16 as one example). If you look at the various kingdoms and nations of this world, you will see a trend: no one individual does it all by themselves. Rather, the different rulers of the different kingdoms and nations will appoint individuals they trust to aid them in governing the people of the kingdom or nation. This is also true with the Kingdom of God.

The first vital thing we must look at is God appoints those whom He trusts. God will never appoint anyone to a position if He cannot trust them first. Jesus said, "One who is faithful in a very little is also faithful in much, and one who is dishonest (unfaithful) in a very little is also dishonest in much" (Luke 16:10). Or, in other words, you prove your trustworthiness (or lack thereof) by how you live for God. If you are unfaithful (inconsistent) in the foundational things that make up a relationship with God, then He will never trust you enough to appoint you to a position of service in His Kingdom. What are the things which God looks at to determine trust?

First, God looks to the individual's private devotion to Him. What constitutes private devotion? The basic things are prayer, reading His Word, worship, fasting, and giving (tithes and offerings). Let's begin by looking at prayer.

Kristopher David Grepke

Prayer

Prayer is our communication with God. The Prophet Jeremiah under divine inspiration said this: "Call to me and I will answer you and tell you great and hidden things that you have not known" (Jeremiah 33:3). Jeremiah makes it plain: first, we are to call, and then He will answer. There is not a more basic definition of communication. More than that though, we also see that it is only in prayer that God reveals "great and hidden things." The deeper we go in prayer, the deeper He reveals and unfolds.

We so often get it wrong with prayer, we think it is only for times when it is necessary or needed. Only in times of trouble or hurt. Such an idea goes against the very teaching of Scripture. Paul said it like this, "Pray without ceasing" (I Thessalonians 5:17). Also, "Continue steadfastly in prayer" (Colossians 4:2). Jesus Himself made it very clear that we are to pray faithfully: "And when you pray, you must not be like the hypocrites. For they love to pray in the synagogues and on the street corners, that they may be seen by others. Truly, I say to you, they have their reward. But when you pray, go into your room and shut the door and pray to your Father who is in secret. And your Father who sees in secret will reward you. And when you pray, do not heap up empty phrases as the Gentiles do, for they think that they will be heard for their many words" (Matthew 6:5-7). Then in the Gospel of Luke, it is recorded, "And He told them a parable to the effect that they ought always to pray and not lose heart" (Luke 18:1).

To abandon faithfulness in prayer is to abandon all hope of you traversing the rough terrain called life. For Jesus said, "Apart from me you can do nothing" (John 15:5). Also, the Lord declared through the Prophet Amos, "Seek me and live" (Amos 5:4). "Seek" there is "darash" in Hebrew, meaning "seek; consult; inquire of." Therefore, our level of living and our quality of life is determined by the level at

Kingdom Progression

which we seek, consult, and inquire of God. Even looking to Jesus as our example, God manifested in the flesh, our Savior. It says of Him, "But he would withdraw to desolate places and pray" (Luke 5:16). The tense of that sentence is plural, meaning He did so often. If He had to get away from the noise often to pray, how much more do we need to?

One crucial thing we have to understand about prayer that is so often misunderstood is that it is not you coming to God asking Him for all the things that you desire for yourself. This goes against many individuals' way of thinking about prayer. Jesus said, "If you ask me anything in my name, I will do it" (John 14:14). This Scripture does not mean that we can throw the Name of Jesus around and get whatever we desire. Rather, it refers to being submitted to the Lordship of Christ and His Will. It refers to one who has sought His Will and is praying for what He has revealed. James declares the same truth (see James 4:3). We do not receive what we ask for in prayer due to asking out of wrong motives: i.e. motives that lie outside of His Will. And John, in his first epistle, makes it plain: "And this is the confidence that we have toward Him, that if we ask anything according to His Will He hears us" (I John 5:14).

Also, we ought not to look at prayer as an obligation but rather as an invitation. The author of Hebrews said it like this: "Let us then with confidence draw near to the throne of grace, that we may receive mercy and find grace to help in time of need" (Hebrews 4:16). Prayer is an invitation to come before the throne of God Himself. When we do, we receive His mercy and His grace. However, to receive these things we must accept the invitation.

Reading His Word

Then there is reading His Word. God spoke this to Joshua: "This Book of the Law shall not depart from your mouth, but you shall meditate on it day and night, so that you may be careful to do according to all that is written in it. For then you will make your way prosperous, and then you will have good success" (Joshua 1:8). The Word of God is essential to any man or woman, not just hoping to be used by God, but for anyone wishing simply to know God. Jesus declared this: "If you abide in my word, you are truly my disciples" (John 8:31). Meaning, if we even want to be able to claim that we are followers of Him, we must be in His Word.

Furthermore, we cannot look at His Word so casually, thinking it is a chore to read. We must firmly grasp the mentality that Jesus conveyed when tempted in the wilderness, "Man shall not live on bread alone, but on every word that comes from the mouth of God" (Matthew 4:4). We must get to a place of desiring His Word more than our physical food. We must desire spiritual nourishment over physical nourishment (this plays into fasting which we will get to momentarily). Job conveyed this same mentality: "I have not departed from the commandments of his lips; I have treasured the words of his mouth more than my portion of food" (Job 23:12). Also, we cannot try and pick and choose Scripture, having the mentality that only portions of it are relevant for us today since we live in a different culture and time. This goes against the very teaching of the Bible, for Paul declared, "All Scripture is breathed out by God and profitable for teaching, for reproof, for correction, for training in righteousness, that the man of God may be complete, equipped for every good work" (II Timothy 3:16-17). At the time Paul wrote this letter to Timothy, the New Testament was not yet formed. Meaning, when Paul said "all Scripture" he was specifically referring to the Old Testament. To further this idea, Paul also said, "For whatever was written in former days was written for our instruction, that through endurance and through the encouragement of the Scriptures we might have hope" (Romans 15:4).

Without His Word, we have no wisdom, no guidance,

Kingdom Progression

and no clarity. The psalmist declared, "Your word is a lamp to my feet, and a light to my path" (Psalms 119:105). I don't have time to go through it all here, but I would implore anyone and everyone to go through and read and study Psalms 119. If you do so with the right heart, you won't be able to walk away from it without having fallen more in love with the Word. "How can a young man keep his way pure? By guarding it according to your word. With my whole heart I seek you; let me not wander from your commandments! I have stored up your word in my heart, that I might not sin against you" (Psalms 119:9-11). Without His Word we cannot know Him, no matter how much we pray. For His Word is God revealed, "In the beginning was the word, and the word was with God, and the word was God" (John 1:1).

I mentioned briefly when mentioning prayer that we need to seek out the Will of God to pray the Will of God. Well, how does one discover His Will? By His Word. Embedded in His Word is the fullness of His Will, but we must come to the Word with our whole hearts with a pang of true hunger, not just chore and ritual if we are to truly receive and perceive.

Worship

We are called to worship God. The well-known psalm declares, "Praise the LORD! Praise God in his sanctuary; praise him in his mighty heavens! Praise him for his mighty deeds; praise him according to his excellent greatness! Praise him with the trumpet sound; praise him with lute and harp! Praise him with the tambourine and dance; praise him with strings and pipe! Praise him with sounding cymbals; praise him with loud clashing cymbals! Let everything that has breath praise the LORD! Praise the LORD!" (Psalms 150:1-6). Two things stand out from this passage: one, as verse six declares, "everything that has breath praise the LORD." Everything is expected to give Him praise and glory and honor. Jesus declared: "I tell you, if these were silent, the very stones would cry out" (Luke 19:40). Two, the psalmist said that we are to "praise Him according to His excellent greatness." Meaning our level of praise declares how great we think He is. The more praise and worship you offer up, the greater you declare Him to be. On the flip side of this, if one withholds such, they declare that they think little of Him. It also is declared in Psalms: "Ascribe to the LORD the glory due his name; worship the LORD in the splendor of holiness" (Psalms 29:2). When worshipping God according to how great we think He is, that level of worship affects more than what is realized. For how great you think God is, according to your praise, is intertwined with faith. The greater the faith you have in God, the greater He can do in you and through you. If your praise (and thereby your faith) is lacking, you hold back God from working in your life to the level which He desires.

However, it is of vital importance that our worship be heartfelt. We cannot go through the motions of "worship" and think that qualifies as an adequate offering of praise. Jesus declared by quoting the Prophet Isaiah: "You hypocrites! Well did Isaiah prophesy of you, when he said: 'This people honors me with their lips, but their heart is far from me; in vain do they worship me, teaching as doctrines the commandments of men'" (Matthew 15:7-9). If our worship is not heartfelt, it is not only in vain, but it is hypocrisy. When we come before God, our minds must be set on Him, thinking of all the wondrous things He has done for us, and our hearts must be filled with thanksgiving and love. When we take those remembrances and deep things of the heart and express them unto God, only then is it true worship. Singing a "worship song" while your mind is on a million other things is not worship, it is a vain routine that God takes no pleasure in. God delights in intentionality.

Kingdom Progression

Fasting

Fasting is just as crucial but often so overlooked. I would not hesitate to say that fasting has become the most overlooked biblical discipline, which is saying something due to the famine of genuine prayer and intentional reading of His Word. Many think of fasting as optional, just an extra thing that "super-Christians" do but isn't for everyone. This is not the case at all. Look to the words of Jesus: "And when you fast, do not look gloomy like the hypocrites, for they disfigure their faces that their fasting may be seen by others. Truly, I say to you, they have received their reward. But when you fast, anoint your head and wash your face, that your fasting may not be seen by others but by your Father who is in secret. And your Father who sees in secret will reward you" (Matthew 6:16-18). We can see two prominent things from this passage: one, when referring to fasting, Jesus said, "when," implying that it is expected from us. Two, we are not to make it known or obvious that we are fasting, for fasting ought to be a private, personal affair between you and God. If you do it for any other reason or motive, it is not genuine, and God will not accept it.

Generally, when we think of fasting, we think of abstaining from food, and this is the most prevalent form of fasting and also the most effective, as you are denying a need of the body. I also think it is good to note that food is not the only thing that can be fasted. I think anything in your life that is a roadblock or a hindrance or a distraction ought to be fasted. If technology is consuming your time, fast it. If entertainment is, fast it. If any sort of secular activity is, fast it.

It is also of vital importance to note that fasting must be done purposefully. Ezra recorded this: "Then I proclaimed a fast there at the river of Ahava, that we might humble ourselves before our God, to seek from Him a safe journey for ourselves, our children, and all our goods...So we fasted and implored our God for this, and he answered our entreaty" (Ezra 8:21,23). If you are abstaining from food but are not being purposeful and intentionally seeking God about a particular issue, then all you have done is make yourself hungry. When we take away food, we ought to fill the time that we would be eating with prayer and His Word instead. If we are not seeking Him more intently and purposefully during our fast, then we have gained nothing. I think it is important to be led by God in our fasts, but I also think it is important that we are disciplined about it. I believe it is good for those wishing to grow in God that they fast at least once a week.

It is important to mention the "why" of fasting. To put it simply, it is to get you out of the way. Before the beginning of Jesus' earthly ministry, even though He was God incarnate, He was led into the wilderness to fast for forty days and forty nights (see Matthew 4:2). Even though He was God incarnate He still came and dwelt in flesh. Thus being the case, He had to submit the flesh in which He dwelt to the Spirit of God within Him. We see a similar event in the life of Moses. God had given him the Ten Commandments up on Mount Sinai (for the second time) and during this time of the renewed covenant, Moses fasted for forty days and forty nights (see Exodus 34:28). Since he was dealing directly with the express Word of God unto the people, he needed to get himself out of the way so that God could speak as He so desired. To ensure it would be His Word, not Moses'.

Giving of Tithes and Offerings

Then there is giving. Giving is crucial. It is important to understand that everything belongs to God because He created all things (see I Corinthians 10:26; Psalms 24:1; Exodus 19:5; and Job 41:11). However, just in case we tried to create a loop-hole, God also declared, "'the silver is mine, and the gold is mine,' declares the LORD of hosts" (Haggai

Kingdom Progression

2:8). We are simply stewards of what ultimately belongs to Him. In Matthew 25:14-30, Jesus gives us the Parable of the Talents. The key points we receive from this parable are, one, God blessed the three individuals by giving to them their talents; two, God expected them to use what they had been given for His gain and glory; three, He blessed those who used what they had been given in a way that glorified Him; and four, He took away the talent from the one who did nothing with it, or worse, used it for secular things since the text says that he hid the talent in the earth (world), and then God gave the talent to one who had used theirs for Him. Therefore, the one was left with nothing.

Malachi said this: "Will a man rob God? Yet you are robbing me. But you say, 'How have we robbed you?' In your tithes and contributions (offerings). You are cursed with a curse, for you are robbing me, the whole nation of you. Bring the full tithe into the storehouse, that there may be food in my house. And thereby put me to the test, says the LORD of hosts, if I will not open the windows of heaven for you and pour down for you a blessing until there is no more need" (Malachi 3:8-10). One, God expects the tithe and offering. A tithe is ten percent. Why does God expect ten percent? Because everything belongs to Him, and we are simply blessed to have been given what we have, and He asks for just a small portion of it back. He also expects the offering. The offering is anything given on top of the ten percent. The offering is often defined as sacrificial. The true definition of sacrifice is to offer up something meaningful or important to you. Two, if we do not give of our tithe and offering, we will be cursed by our hand. Three, if we are faithful in our tithe and offering, we will be blessed in a manner by which "we will not have room enough to receive it" (as the NASB words it).

It is also important to understand what exactly is to be tithed. Proverbs 3:9-10 states, "Honor the LORD with your wealth and with the firstfruits of all your produce;

then your barns will be filled with plenty, and your vats will be bursting with wine." Meaning, we are to tithe off our first fruits. Meaning, as soon as the increase comes in, the tithe immediately comes off. Before the IRS and State Government take their share, God must be first given His share. For the increase came from Him, so He ought to be honored before the rest.

We must also understand that we cannot be bitter or resentful in our giving, for God will not accept that, and we will be cursed the same. Paul said: "Each one must give as he has decided in his heart, not reluctantly or under compulsion, for God loves a cheerful giver" (II Corinthians 9:7). There is a quote that I love from the book "The Gift of Giving" by Wayne Watts that says, "There are three kinds of giving: grudge giving, duty giving, and thanksgiving. Grudge giving says, 'I have to': duty giving says, 'I ought to'; thanksgiving says, 'I want to.'"

Private and Corporate Devotion

Something of importance to note: all five of these things listed can be done on a corporate (Church Body) level. You can engage in times of prayer with the Body, times of reading His Word with the Body, unite in worship with the Body, participate is a unified fast across the Body, and unified giving with the Body. Two general principles lead me to identify these things specifically as private devotions: one, if you neglect to engage faithfully in these things on a private level, you're not going to engage in them on the Body level. If you don't pray in private, you won't pray with the Body, or if you do, it will be half-hearted and vain repetition, which God detests and compares to paganism (see Matthew 6:7). If you don't read the Word on a private level, you may do so when the man or woman of God gets up to speak, but your heart will not be engaged. If you don't worship God privately, your corporate worship will be in vain. If you don't

Kingdom Progression

fast on a private level, you will be more concerned about yourself and your flesh than the desires of God and the needs of the Body. Also, if you don't give faithfully, you will not stand up and commit to meeting needs in the moment. What you do in private will show by how you engage corporately. Two, these things ought to be kept private unless they are specifically done on a corporate level. Even when done on a corporate level, they should not be flaunted. Jesus said this: "Beware of practicing your righteousness before other people in order to be seen by them, for then you will have no reward from your Father who is in heaven" (Matthew 6:1). All that we do is to be for Him, not ourselves. "And whatever you do, in word or deed, do everything in the name of the Lord Jesus, giving thanks to God the Father through him" (Colossians 3:17).

After looking at an individual's private devotion, God looks at an individual's corporate devotion. As I mentioned before, all the things listed for private devotion can be done on a corporate level. However, I will take that one step further here and say, all these things ought to be done also on a corporate level. It can't be stated enough that these things must first exist on a private level, for if they don't exist on a private level then they won't exist on a corporate level. Or if they do "exist" on a corporate level, it will be fake and routine, vanity. Many think they only need one or the other, a strong private level of devotion, or a strong corporate level of devotion.

First, the idea that we can survive on our own goes against the very teaching of Scripture. The author of Hebrews said, "not neglecting to meet together, as is the habit of some, but encouraging one another, and all the more as you see the Day drawing near" (Hebrews 10:25). Meaning, our level of faithfulness and devotion to the Body should not ever become less over time, but in actuality it should grow and become greater and stronger as time draws ever closer to the end. Paul tells us why this is so crucial in I Corinthians 12:12-27. First, Paul tells us that the Body is made up of many different members, drawing allusion to the human body. The human body is not all one member or function, but rather it is made up of many different aspects that all work together in unity. Each part of the human body is crucial to the overall function of the body. This is also how it is with the Body of Christ. We are all different but are all crucial to the proper function of the Body. Then he goes beyond that and states that an individual part of the human body cannot operate on its own. Paul said it like this: "The eye cannot say to the hand, 'I have no need of you,' nor again the head to the feet, 'I have no need of you'" (I Corinthians 12:21). The eye cannot exist without the hand, for the eye cannot function in the same capacity as the hand. Same with head and feet. The head cannot exist without the feet, for the head cannot move as the feet can. No individual aspect can exist on its own. You're a hand? On your own, you will have no sight or ability to move. You're an eye? You can see but can do nothing about what you see. We were created to come alongside the rest of the Body and operate with them. As Paul said: "From whom the whole body, joined and held together by every joint with which it is equipped, when each part is working properly, makes the body grow so that it builds itself up in love" (Ephesians 4:16).

    We also cannot simply have corporate devotion and no private devotion. As I said, this is a vain routine. Under the inspiration of God, the Apostle John said this: "I know your works, your labor, your patience, and that you cannot bear those who are evil. And you have tested those who say they are apostles and are not, and have found them liars; and you have persevered and have patience, and have labored for My name's sake and have not become weary. Nevertheless I have this against you, that you have left your first love" (Revelation 2:2-4 NASB). Jesus was conveying how busy they had been with the work of the Church. He attributed to them those who, work, labor, have patience, detest evil, test the integrity of those who claim to work for God, and have not grown weary in all their work. Many would look at this list and think this was a powerful Church. Then we look to the next Scripture, and God declares that amidst all this, they had forgotten the most important thing: their First Love. Or in other words, Him. They had become so busy working in and for the Church that they had neglected their private devotion. All that we do for the Church means nothing if we have no private devotion to God, or in other words, if we have no relationship with God. "But the LORD said to Samuel, 'Do not look on his appearance or on the height of his stature, because I have rejected him. For the LORD sees not as man sees: man looks on the outward appearance, but the LORD looks on the heart'" (I Samuel 16:7). What good is it to be devoted to the house but not to the God of the house? We ought to be careful that we do not replace Jesus as our God by allowing the building to become our god.

Serving the Church

Along with these, one ought to also be faithful in service to the church. Don't be confused, I am not referring here to the individual's gifting. Think of it like this: we are all called to serve (work for) His Church, but we all also ought to serve the church by dedicating our time and talents. Paul said this: "For you were called to freedom, brothers. Only do not use your freedom as an opportunity for the flesh, but through love serve one another. For the whole Law is fulfilled in one word, 'You shall love your neighbor as yourself'" (Galatians 5:13-14). He said again, later in the chapter: "So then, as we have opportunity, let us do good to everyone, and especially to those who are of the household of faith" (Galatians 6:10). Also, Solomon wrote this: "Whoever brings blessing will be enriched, and one who waters will himself be watered" (Proverbs 11:25).

I mentioned it above regarding giving tithes and

offerings, but the Parable of the Talents (see Matthew 25:14-30) can also be applied to serving. For we all know that we were all gifted with some talent. There is an array of talents one might have, singing, playing an instrument, design, art (in the classic sense), and so on. These talents were not given to us to simply use for ourselves, or to use for the world, but these gifts were given to us by God, so we ought to use these gifts for Him. We do this by using them in the church. If you can play an instrument, play it for God. If you can sing, sing for God. If you are a warm, hospitable person, be that for God by being a greeter. These are only a few examples. If you have a gift and talent, use it for God. However, don't try to flaunt yourself by displaying your talent. Don't try and get up and play an instrument in a way that will make people honor you. Don't sing in a manner that brings you praise and not God. When you greet, don't make it about you, make it about God. "Whatever you do, work heartily, as for the Lord and not for men, knowing that from the Lord you will receive the inheritance as your reward. You are serving the Lord Christ" (Colossians 3:23-24).

    If we use what God has given us, He will bless us for it. If we dedicate our time and talents to the church, He will pour back out onto us. As Solomon said, and as Jesus said in His parable, those who bless will be blessed in return, and those who water will be watered. Those who work for Him will be given more. Paul, in Galatians again, also said, "Do not be deceived: God is not mocked, for whatever one sows, that will he also reap" (Galatians 6:7).

    These do not make up the totality of all that God looks at. There are a few other things that we must understand when it comes to God's level of trust toward us. One of the most crucial aspects of one's walk with God is faith.

Faith

    Faith is an integral aspect of an individual's walk with

Kingdom Progression

God, not just one in ministry but one seeking to know God in any manner. The author of Hebrews states, "And without faith it is impossible to please him, for whoever would draw near to God must believe that he exists and that he rewards those who seek him" (Hebrews 11:6). Where faith is absent there is a lack of pleasing aroma that draws God unto you. Whoever would desire to know God (draw near to God) must believe (have faith) that He exists and that He rewards those who seek Him. This idea here of seeking Him is not a simple game of trivial hide and seek. This word "seek" is complex, "ekzēteō," and it refers to seeking after carefully and diligently. Webster's Dictionary defines "diligent" as, "constant in effort or exertion to accomplish what is undertaken; prosecuted with care and constant effort." Therefore, faith must be coupled with sincere, intentional, heartfelt seeking.

We will come back, momentarily, to faith being unified with action. First, we need to understand what faith is exactly. In the first verse of the same chapter quoted above, the author of Hebrews said, "Now faith is the assurance of things hoped for, the conviction of things not seen" (Hebrews 11:1). Let's break this Scripture down to develop a proper understanding of faith. First, we see the word "assurance." This is a very powerful word in Greek, it is "hupostasis." "Hupostasis" holds a variety of meanings, all very powerful when examined in the context of this Scripture. Some of its meanings are the foundation, the true nature (makeup; identity) of a thing, and steadfastness of mind. Faith, then, is the groundwork. Faith is what we stand upon. Furthermore, faith is also the very thing that makes up who we are. It is our identity. Faith is also what gives us the strength to stand strong in our minds amid doubt.

The hope mentioned here in Hebrews and throughout the Bible is not what we define hope as today. We define hope as simply an optimistic viewpoint. However, hope here, "elpizō," truly means "expectation." Faith, then, is the foundation of expectation that we stand upon. Expectation is what makes up the core of who we are. Expectation is what conquers all doubt to give us steadfastness of mind.

Then the author of Hebrews continues by stating that faith is a "conviction." This is very interesting, for a conviction is something that grips you. Take for example, when God convicts one of their sins. That conviction so grips them that one of two things will happen: one, they will either run as far away as possible to avoid its gripping power, or two, they will run to an alter in repentance. What is seen, then, is that faith isn't something we necessarily hold, faith is something that grabs hold of us. What grabs hold of us is the expectation of things not seen, or not yet manifested. This is why Paul admonished us to "Walk by faith and not by sight" (II Corinthians 5:7).

Returning to the idea that faith is coupled with action: James, in his epistle, properly defines what faith looks like. In James 2:14-16 he gives several examples of how simple words do not fix dire situations. You see someone hungry and say to them, "Go and be filled," yet give them no food. What good have you done? None. Faith works the same. James said it like this, "So also faith by itself, if it does not have works, is dead" (James 2:17). What James is conveying here is that it is easy to simply say something. It is easy to say, "I believe." One whose heart is full of disbelief can utter those words and those around them would have no idea that they're lying if they did not judge their words according to their actions. True faith is only present when obedience is coupled with it. Obedience must be the response to true faith or else faith is not true.

Obedience

It is important to understand that God and His Word are not two separate things, but rather, one (see John 1:1). To claim obedience to God, but not obey all His Word is a pure

Kingdom Progression

contradiction. "But this command I gave them: 'Obey my voice, and I will be your God, and you shall be my people. And walk in all the way that I command you, that it may be well with you" (Jeremiah 7:23). Also, "If you love me, you will keep my commandments (Word of God)" (John 14:15). And again, "But he said, 'Blessed rather are those who hear the word of God and keep it!'" (Luke 11:28). And once more, "Why do you call me 'Lord, Lord,' and do not what I tell you?" (Luke 6:46). Scripture is clear on this matter: if we do not obey His Word (thereby obeying Him), we cannot claim Him to be our Lord, nor will He be our God.

"Lord," in Luke 6:46, is "kurios" in Greek, meaning, "a person who exercises absolute ownership rights." Meaning, you cannot claim to be devoted and faithful to God unless there is obedience. If we look back to Jeremiah 7:23, God admonishes us to "walk in all the ways that I have commanded you." I have heard different individuals make the statement that they are looking for the "doctrine" that best suits them and their personalities and lifestyle. Such a statement spits in the face of all that the Bible is. The only true doctrine is the entirety of the Word of God. Paul affirms this truth to us: "All Scripture is inspired (or breathed out, meaning it came from His mouth) by God and beneficial for teaching, for rebuke, for correction, for training in righteousness; so that the man or woman of God may be fully capable, equipped for every good work" (II Timothy 3:16-17 NASB). And again, "For everything (the totality) that was written in the past was written for our instruction, so that through endurance and the encouragement of the Scriptures, we might have hope" (Romans 15:4). Paul also stressed the importance of not perverting or changing His Word in any way (see Galatians 1:6-9). He so wanted to stress the importance of this that he made the same statement twice: "As we have said before, so now I say again: If anyone is preaching to you a gospel contrary to the one you received, let him be accursed" (Galatians 1:9). "Gospel" is the Greek word "euaggélion" which does not explicitly refer to the life, death, burial, and resurrection of Jesus, but includes the entire Bible. It is not limited to how one is saved. "Accursed" is "anathema" which is "something given up to destruction." The same warning is given to us by the Apostle John in The Book of Revelation (see Revelation 22:18-19). He states that anyone who takes away from or adds to what has been written, their name will be taken out of the Book of Life.

To say that obedience is not crucial is as severe an understatement as one could make. Malachi wrote this under the inspiration of God: "For I the LORD do not change" (Malachi 3:6a). The author of Hebrews said the same thing, "Jesus Christ is the same yesterday and today, and forever" (Hebrews 13:8). We have already mentioned how God and His Word are the same, so if He does not change, then His Word does not change. Therefore, what was true back then is true today. Therefore, obedience to the totality of His Word is crucial.

As vital as obedience is, we cannot merely look at obedience as an obligation. To look at obedience in such a manner is what causes so many to stumble and fall. The Apostle John said this: "Loving God means keeping his commandments, and his commandments are not burdensome" (I John 5:3 NLT). This reflects one of the earlier Scriptures I quoted, "If you love me, you will keep my commandments" (John 14:15). Love must be the driving force behind obedience, or else it is in vain. John stated that when love is at the center of obedience, His Word is not burdensome. That, therefore, indicates that if love is not at the center of obedience, His Word does become burdensome. One can only carry a burden for so long before they drop it.

Submission

The author of Hebrews declared this: "Obey your leaders and submit to them, for they are keeping watch over

Kingdom Progression

your souls, as those who will have to give an account. Let them do this with joy and not with groaning, for that would be of no advantage to you" (Hebrews 13:17). Several things are important to understand: all are called to submit to a leader (spiritual head or covering). Notice, the author does not specify who ought to submit. They did not say, "the saints of the church," or, "the more immature, irresponsible saints that need babysitting," or any such thing. They simply said, submit. However, to truly narrow down who exactly was the target audience, the author said, "Let's" (v.15). "Let's" is short for "let us," and "us" is plural, all inclusive. We are all admonished to submit to those who God has placed over us.

One may try and argue that the author is referring to submitting to earthly authority, as in government, and there are plenty Scriptures about just that (see Romans 13:1-7). This passage is not referring to such. For the author specifically states that these leaders "watch out for your souls" and will "give account" for you to God. These are our spiritual leaders that keep watch over us to make sure that we do not go astray. As I said, all are called to submit, no matter how "lofty" in the Kingdom you become. Although, if you are dwelling in "loftiness," I would surmise that you have left sight of His Kingdom and have become consumed with your kingdom. We will come back to that.

There are two things of great importance that I feel we must examine. One, what is submission? If we do not properly define submission, then we will all go around creating our own ideas and definitions. "Submission" is "hupeikó," which means "to yield to; to submit to; to surrender; to become weak." I feel that "to become weak" conveys this most powerfully. It is not describing one that is forced into weakness, rather, "to become weak" is to make one's self weak. Meaning, it is to lay down your strong stubbornness, from which you try (and fail) to rule your own life, and instead, willingly give it to another. A good example of this would be if you had a major life decision to make that would affect multiple aspects of your life. Instead of taking it unto yourself to make this decision, you go to your spiritual covering and ask them for their counsel. The true state of one's level of submission is revealed when the answer that is given by the spiritual covering is not the answer that is desired by the one who asks. Are you willing to yield and make yourself weak to the guidance of your covering?

Two, for a moment, imagine yourself at a level of sovereign rule over a people. You are going to appoint others to help you govern the people. Would you appoint someone to help govern the people that was not submitted to you? No. Neither would God. God spoke this to Saul through the Prophet Samuel: "For rebellion is as the sin of divination, and presumption is as iniquity and idolatry. Because you have rejected the word of the LORD, he has also rejected you from being king" (I Samuel 15:23). "Divination" is "qesem" in Hebrew, meaning, more accurately, "witchcraft." "Presumption" is "patsar," meaning "stubbornness." Therefore, Saul had become rebellious and stubborn, equating to witchcraft, wickedness (iniquity), and idolatry (meaning he had put other things before God; in this case, it was himself, and his desires). Because of these things, God refused ("ma'ac" or "rejected" as it is worded in the Scripture) to let Saul operate in a place of leadership over His people.

Character

Another aspect we must examine (when it comes to God's level of trust in someone) is their character. In I Timothy 3 (using the NASB as the reference here), the Apostle Paul gives us a list of qualities that need to be present in one wishing to serve as an "overseer" (he gives a similar, but less extensive list, in Titus 1). Some may dismiss this list because they think it only applies to this one specific role, but an examination of this word thwarts such thinking. This

Kingdom Progression

word is "episkopos," which refers to "one called by God to provide personalized, first-hand care and protection for His flock." I would argue that this description applies to every single ministry and office. For if you are not caring for or protecting His flock, then what are you doing? Because even if you are not directly working with an individual to care for and protect them, all that you do for God and His Church (flock) should be done through the mindset and motivation of care and protection. Therefore, all who serve in any capacity ought to align with this list given by Paul.

First, Paul gives the quality of being "above reproach." This is "anepilémptos," referring to "one who cannot be found secretly doing something evil, wicked, sinful, or unrighteous." Essentially, one whose "hands are clean," as the expression goes. This does not mean that one must be perfect, having never sinned, for God to trust them. We know that "All have sinned and fall short of the glory of God" (Romans 3:23). Also, "If we say we have no sin, we deceive ourselves, and the truth is not in us" (I John 1:8). This is a call to faithful morality (the morality being according to God's standards).

Next is having "one spouse," and this is of course of the opposite gender, as Paul put it: "the husband of one wife." This may seem like a silly thing to put into a list of character requirements. What Paul is conveying here is much deeper than initially realized. Paul is implying here that one be devoted and faithful to one spouse. Again, this may seem trivial. However, Jesus said in Matthew 5:28 that if one looks lustfully at another, they've committed adultery in their heart. Therefore, what Paul is pointing to is one who is free from lust. One who does not look at others in lust but looks through eyes of purity.

Then he states that one is to be "sober-minded." This is "néphalios," and it means "free from life-dominating influences." Naturally, our minds go to the big ones: drugs, alcohol, and pornography. However, if given space and time, anything can become a life-dominating influence. To put it plainly, this one is free from idolatry. One who keeps God first as their focus and doesn't allow anything else to dictate their lives. This can be technology, entertainment, shopping, overall materialism, and things like these.

"Self-controlled" is the next thing Paul lists. This is "sóphrón" in Greek, and it describes "being well-balanced from God's perspective." It describes an individual who does not command themselves but rather gives command of themselves to God. This is much deeper than self-control as we often think of it. It is more so a level of deep submission that brings about biblical balance. Next is "respectable," which is "kosmios." "Respectable" is the best, most accurate translation of this word. To define "respectable" would be "regarded by society to be good, proper, and/or correct" (Oxford Languages).

One wishing to be called to serve must also be "hospitable." "Philoxenos" is the Greek word here. "Love" and "generosity" are directly connected to this word, along with "hospitality." Having a welcoming attitude bathed in loving generosity is at the heart of every true servant. One must also be "able to teach." This is "didaktikos," which simply means "skillful in teaching." The question then arises, "What if I'm not called to be a Teacher?" To limit this qualification in such a manner is to read the text in a much too narrow-minded way. For to be "able to teach" thereby requires knowledge and understanding of the thing being taught, so that is one thing it implies: having knowledge and understanding of God. Also, the very basic definition of teaching is being able to bring about understanding (because if your listeners did not grow in understanding, all you did was babel). No matter the office or ministry, if someone asked you a biblical question, should you not be able to answer it? And if you answer it and helped bring about understanding, are you not teaching?

Then there is "not a drunkard." This is "paroinos"

and it refers to "any sort of addiction to mind-altering influences." Drugs and alcohol are the big things here. Many believe that drinking itself is not wrong, only being drunk is a sin. This is an attempt to find a loophole in Scripture. I do not have time to go into all of it here, but I would encourage all to study "wine" mentioned throughout the Bible. Here is a summary of what you will find: one, "wine" can refer to unfermented and fermented grape juice; two, in most places where "wine" is referred to as fermented juice it is associated with a bad chain of events; three, understanding the cultural applications of "wine" in the time of the Bible is crucial. You will discover that alcohol, as we know it today, was not how it was back then. Plus, even when wine was fermented, they would dilute it with water so it would not affect them in negative ways. Four, even the slightest bit of alcohol in our day and age affects you. To say you can drink with no negative side effects is pure denial.

"Not violent" is next and it is "pléktés." This refers to "one who intentionally seeks out fights." Rather, we are called to be "gentle." "Gentle" is "epiekés" and an example of such a person is "one who seeks to fulfill the spirit (true intent) of the Law, not the letter (condemning) of the Law." Also, we are to be "peaceable." This is "amachos," and it refers to "one who does not engage in pointless fights." This would include theological debates. We are not called to debate the Gospel but proclaim it. If one does not wish to hear what we have to say, we are to "shake off the dust from your feet when you leave that house or town" (Matthew 10:14b).

Then we are told to be "not a lover of money." This is "aphilarhuros" in Greek and simply means "not a materialist." This one has the potential to cut many very deep. Materialism has become such an issue in America. We are consumed by material gain. We want all the new and best things available, even if we don't need them. This mindset has, unfortunately, crept into the church. We must get back to the proper understanding: "Do not love the world or the things in the world. If anyone loves the world, the love of the Father is not in him" (I John 2:15). We have attempted to spiritualize materialism, buying the newest, most expensive shoes to wear Sunday because we are "honoring God." More accurately we are seeking the attention of those around us. Also, buying new, fancy Bibles with much commentary and study notes, attempting to appear spiritual. It means nothing for you to have a Study Bible if you do not study it. I digress.

After this extensive list of qualifications, Paul gives one last brief statement on the character of one wishing to serve. In this passage, Paul uses "he." This should not discourage any women from thinking they cannot be called, for we read of many different women in roles of leadership (Deborah: Judges 4-5; Esther; Phoebe: Romans 16:1; Priscilla: Acts 18:26; etc.). Rather, the "he" Paul used should be understood as a general term used for all.

Paul said this: "He must manage his own household well, with all dignity keeping his children submissive, for if someone does not know how to manage his own household, how will he care for God's church? He must not be a recent convert, or he may become puffed up with conceit and fall into the condemnation of the devil. Moreover, he must be well thought of by outsiders, so that he may not fall into disgrace, into a snare of the devil" (I Timothy 3:4-7 NASB). There are a few things I feel the need to expound upon here. One thing my Pastor (Pastor Brian Lane) says is, "Before the Church can be right, the home has to be right." As stated above, corporate devotion means nothing and equates to nothing if there is no private devotion. This all coincides with Paul's first statement. Of course, a parent cannot make their child faithful to God, but a parent ought to do all they can to ensure it. The biggest thing a parent can do for their child is to be an example to them as to what it looks and sounds like.

The second statement should not discourage any.

Kingdom Progression

For even Paul waited three years after his experience with Jesus before going to Jerusalem to begin his ministry (see Galatians 1:15-18). Another thing my Pastor says is, "We cannot lead others into an experience we have not had yet ourselves." Jesus Himself said, "And if the blind lead the blind, both will fall into a pit" (Matthew 15:14). We must grow in Him who called us before we attempt to lead others deeper into Him.

Then there is this final statement of Paul's, which can appear confusing. If we are to be separate from the world, why is he admonishing us to "be well thought of by outsiders?" This very simply refers to one who lives a consistently-faithful life both in and out of the church. Through his consistent faithfulness, he will "have a beautiful testimony among them" (as The Passion Translation words verse 7).

The Order of Marriage

When speaking on what God looks at to see if He can trust an individual and trust on the character of one, it is also imperative that we speak on marriage. I subtitled this section "The Order of Marriage" purposefully. It is important to understand that God is a God of order, not chaos, and if we are to operate in the divine Will of God, we must abide in that order.

We see from the very beginning of Creation that God desires order.

> In the beginning, God created the heavens and the earth. The earth was without form and void, and darkness was over the face of the deep. And the Spirit of God was hovering over the face of the waters.
> -Genesis 1:1-2

Where does this passage convey that He desires order? The details lie in the depths of the Hebrew words. We are told that "darkness was over the face of the deep." "Deep" is "tehom," and it is one of the Hebrew words for "water," only it refers to a very specific state of water. "Tehom" refers to water in a state of absolute chaos; it is a very destructive environment in which no life can be sustained. This was the pre-creation state. Then we see a shift when the Spirit of God appeared and "was hovering over the face of the waters." "Waters" here is "mayim," and it refers to life-giving water: life-sustaining. The key to all of this is what brought about the change from chaos to order: the Spirit of God showed up and hovered above. The key to understanding this is the stance His Spirit took: He was above. This implies dominance over, authority over, and control. God showed up, took authoritative control of the chaos, and brought about order.

We see this further upon examination of the order of the Tabernacle (see Exodus 27; 30). We won't go through all of that here, but referencing these things, the author of Hebrews said, "They serve a copy and shadow of the heavenly things. For when Moses was about to erect the tent, he was instructed by God, saying, 'See that you make everything according to the pattern that was shown you on the mountain'" (Hebrews 8:5). The pattern (order) that God conveyed to Moses was a representation of the heavenly order that He desired.

Moving onto the order of marriage, Paul talks in-depth about marriage in Ephesians 5:22-33. Here is what we learn: marriage is meant to be ordered after the pattern of Christ and His Church. What does that mean? Paul conveys that the husband is the head of the wife, even as Christ is the Head of the Church. Thus, being the case, just as the Church submits to Him, the wives ought to also submit to their husbands. This is not to say that the husband has a right to be controlling or be a dictator over her, for when speaking on the

Kingdom Progression

union of a man and woman in marriage, God said, "Therefore a man shall leave his father and his mother and hold fast to his wife, and they shall become one flesh" (Genesis 2:24). "One flesh" refers to a state of complete unity between the two. Meaning, it is not the husband ruling over the wife in a controlling way, but the two coming alongside one another and being in unity. We must understand that there must be a leader, or else chaos would be the result (and God does not abide in chaos as we have said). He appointed the husband to be the head (leader). However, we also misunderstand the idea of submission to authority. We think that by submitting to authority we forsake any authority we might have. The opposite is true. It is only through submission to authority that we have authority. The wife, then, submitting to her husband, walks in a place of intense power and authority.

We are also told by Paul how the husband is to lead his wife and family, that is, by love. He states that just as Christ loves the Church and laid Himself down for her, the husband ought also to do for his wife.

Men also need to understand the importance of their position as the head, and women need to understand the importance of being submissive. We are given an example of what happens when a husband and wife step outside of this divine order, for this is what transpired in the Garden of Eden. What we see is that Eve was tempted by Satan to delve into pride and self-promotion, she gave in to the lie of the enemy, and took the fruit and gave it also to her husband. Meaning, she stepped outside of the order and took the position of the head and made a decision for both of them. We condemn Eve for bringing sin into the world, but we miss an integral part of the story, for it is possible that Adam was sitting there the whole time, watching Eve be tempted. What we see, then, is that Adam first abandoned his role as the head (which should protect and keep watch over his wife and family). By abandoning his role, it then forced Eve to abandon her role, which resulted in the death of them both (see Genesis 3:1-6).

We already begin to see the cruciality of proper order in the marriage, but the Apostle Peter adds to this. He comes alongside the Apostle Paul and echoes the importance of proper order in the marriage, ending his discourse by saying, "So that your prayers may not be hindered" (I Peter 3:7). Not only does improper order in the marriage birth death and destruction, but it also causes your prayers to be hindered. This word "hindered" is "ekkoptō" and it means, "to cut off." Improper order cuts off your prayers before they even reach the throne room of God.

Abiding in the proper order of marriage is imperative in the life of one wishing to even have a relationship with God, let alone desiring to be used by God.

Conclusion

Why?

Two questions arise from all of this; the first is, why is all of this so important? Why would God care so deeply about all these things being present in one to judge if He can trust them? Solomon answers this question for us in a very simple manner: "Whoever walks with the wise becomes wise, but the companion of fools will suffer harm" (Proverbs 13:20). To put it in other words, you become like those whom you follow. God knows that whoever is leading His people is an image of what His people will eventually look like. To say that God is careful about whom He appoints is an understatement. Paul said this: "For consider your calling, brothers: not many of you were wise according to worldly standards, not many were powerful, not many were of noble birth. But God chose what is foolish in the world to shame the wise; God chose what is weak in the world to shame the strong; God chose what is low and despised in the world, even things that are not, to bring to nothing things that are, so

Kingdom Progression

that no human being might boast in the presence of God" (I Corinthians 1:26-29). "God chose what is low and despised in the world, even things that are not, to bring to nothing things that are," refers to those who are not built up and of high reputation in the world; rather, those who have been overlooked and viewed as lesser. One could describe these individuals as humble. God does not want His Bride to be puffed up, prideful, conceited, self-centered, or the like. He wants a humble Bride. This will only happen if the leaders themselves are such.

How?

The second question is, how do we know if someone has been truly called by God versus them usurping themselves into a role, as the author of Hebrews said, "and no one takes this honor for himself, but only when called by God, just as Aaron was" (Hebrews 5:4)? Jesus had this to say on the matter: "Beware of false prophets, who come to you in sheep's clothing, but inwardly they are ravenous wolves. You will recognize them by their fruits. Are grapes gathered from thorn bushes, or figs from thistles? So, every healthy tree bears good fruit, but the diseased tree bears bad fruit. A healthy tree cannot bear bad fruit, nor can a diseased tree bear good fruit. Every tree that does not bear good fruit is cut down and thrown into the fire. Thus you will recognize them by their fruits" (Matthew 7:15-20). First, let's examine this word for "false prophets," for it is easy to think that he is only referring to this specific false ministry. However, the Greek word "pseudoprophētés" used here refers to "someone pretending to speak the Word of the Lord but is an imposter." All ministry speaks the Word of the Lord, so this refers to all forms of false ministry. Jesus said that we would recognize these types of false ministries "by their fruit." This will be our focus.

Fruit is the natural by-product of a seed-bearing

organism, such as a tree or bush or the like. The fruit is how the organism reproduces itself. The fruit can also be tainted based on the environment the organism that bore the fruit is planted in. Since the fruit is how the organism reproduces itself, if the fruit is tainted, then what is reproduced will be tainted. On the flip side, if the environment in which the organism is planted is good, then its fruit will be good. If its fruit is good, then what it reproduces will also be good. The question then becomes, how do we know what fruit to look for? In Galatians 5:19-23 Paul gives us two lists conveying two different types of fruits (we discussed these lists in the previous chapter, but they bear mentioning here as well). I am only going to focus on the second of the two lists. Paul refers to these as the "Fruit of the Spirit." These are love, joy, peace, patience, kindness, goodness, faithfulness, gentleness, and self-control. Something of supreme importance that cannot be overlooked: these are the Fruit of the Spirit, the Holy Spirit, aka Jesus Christ Himself. These are not love, joy, peace, patience, kindness, goodness, faithfulness, gentleness, and self-control as humanity defines but rather as God defines. His standard. The question then is, how do we operate in His Fruit? The quality of fruit is determined by the quality of the environment. Therefore, the answer to that question is to be firmly rooted and grounded in Him. Once you have been Born Again and live a life of faithful private and corporate devotion and pursue to live a set apart life unto Him by evidence of your character, then and only then will your environment be right and His Fruit bear evidence in you.

    Why am I not focusing on the first list given by Paul? If you look back at that list, Paul describes it as the works (or fruit) of the flesh. He gives several examples as to what these are, but then ends that list with this, "and things like these" (Galatians 5:21 NASB). That simple phrase tells me that what is listed is not the totality of the fruit of the flesh but rather just some of its fruit. However, no such thing is present in the Fruit of the Spirit list. This tells me that what is listed is the totality of the Fruit of the Spirit. Taking those two things into consideration, here is the conclusion I come to: if you are not operating in the Fruit of the Spirit that Paul listed, then you are therefore operating in the fruit of the flesh.

Clarity

One may read this and think that being constant in these varying areas is impossible. Such a one would be correct. The Prophet Isaiah declared, "We have all become like one who is unclean, and all our righteous deeds are like a polluted garment. We all fade like a leaf, and our iniquities, like the wind, take us away" (Isaiah 64:6). We were born in sin (see Psalms 51:5). Thus, being the case, our flesh is drawn toward sin. On our own, we could never even begin to walk in the level of faithfulness discussed here. This is where many get it wrong, they think God expects them to do it alone. They think that if they can't do it alone, God will therefore cast judgment upon them. They allow condemnation to destroy them. What they forget are the crucial words of Paul, "there is therefore now no condemnation for those who are in Christ Jesus" (Romans 8:1). God does not condemn, He only convicts. Condemnation is a judgment too heavy for one to bear that ultimately destroys the one. Conviction, rather, is God drawing the one into His mercy and grace.

For one to be able to walk in this manner seems impossible. Thankfully, we serve a God that defies the definitions of what is possible. "But Jesus looked at them and said, 'With man this is impossible, but with God all things are possible'" (Matthew 19:26). Not once in all of Scripture are we told that God expects us to do this alone. He stated that if we do not have Him, we therefore have and are nothing (see John 15:5). Paul brings strong clarity to this, "for it is God who works in you, both to will and to work for his good pleasure" (Philippians 2:13).

What many don't understand is that without Him we have no ability in the slightest to walk in holiness or faithfulness. Not just this, without Him our desire to walk in such is lacking if not completely nonexistent. It is His Spirit that works in us to build the desire and give us the ability to walk in a manner that pleases Him.

The multiple aspects of a mature Christian listed in this chapter cannot be looked at merely as "works." We do not endeavor to engage in these things because of religious duty, or if that is the motive, then the motive is wrong. It is not about duty; it is about the relationship. Further, it is only through the power of sincere relationship that one will be kept in alignment with these aspects. As it has been stated, we could never consistently abide in these on our own, but we are completely dependent upon Him and His grace working in us. He enables us by His in-dwelling Spirit and living Word to walk in a manner that pleases Him. If ever religious duty becomes the sole motivator, then God convict us.

A.W. Tozer said it like this in his book, The Pursuit of God, "Private prayer should be practiced by every Christian. Long periods of Bible meditation will purify our gaze and direct it; church attendance will enlarge our outlook and increase our love for others. Service and work and activity; all are good and should be engaged in by every Christian. But at the bottom of all these things, giving meaning to them, will be the inward habit of beholding God."

A personal, real, intimate relationship with Jesus must be at the heart of all that we do for Him, lest all that we do for Him be in vain. Let these words serenade your heart as the content of this chapter saturates your mind.

3
Ministry

Ministry today is widely misunderstood. We have this idea of it that has no basis whatsoever in Scripture. What I aim to do here is to bring about a correct understanding of ministry. To do so, we must first examine what it is not (i.e. how so many think it to be today).

What Ministry is Not

Understanding the proper meaning and image (what it foundationally is and looks like) is crucial because we can only properly operate in ministry if we understand it in its true sense.

Human beings are inherently flawed and sinful. David said it like this: "For I was born a sinner—yes, from the moment my mother conceived me" (Psalms 51:5 NLT). It is this way because of what took place in the Garden of Eden. Humanity was created in the image (likeness) of God (see Genesis 1:26-27). God is not flesh and blood, so we know that being created in His image referred to His character, the inner part of us. This is confirmed in Genesis 2:7, "Then the LORD God formed the man of dust from the ground and breathed into his nostrils the breath of life, and the man became a living creature." God created the flesh of humanity from the dust of the ground. "For dust you are and to dust you shall return" (Genesis 3:19). However, notice in Genesis 2:7 that humanity did not come to life when its flesh was formed. Humanity only came into being after God breathed into him the Breath of Life. The Hebrew word there is "neshamah" and can also mean "wind" or "spirit." We know then that man was created to be a spiritual being that was simply housed in flesh.

The story goes on, as we've discussed previously, God put humanity in the Garden and told them not to eat of that one tree, for on the day that they did, they would die. However, they did eat. Interestingly, they did not drop dead. What happened? Did God lie? Was He attempting to use a scare tactic? No. You see, they did die that day but not physically. They died spiritually. On that day there was a divide created between humanity and divinity, between flesh and Spirit. Ever since that day, we have been living in that divide. Even those of us who have been filled with His Spirit, still struggle with that divide between flesh and Spirit. Each one of us struggles with the temptations of this sinful world, as James put it, "But each person is tempted when he is lured and enticed by his desire. Then desire when it has conceived gives birth to sin, and sin when it is fully grown brings forth death" (James 1:14-15). I say all of this to simply emphasize the truth that we all struggle to forsake the lusts of our flesh.

Primarily, when we think of or hear about lust, our minds automatically go to sins of a sexual nature. However, this improper understanding limits the true scope of this word. "Epithymía" is the Greek for "lust," and it simply means, "passion built on strong feelings." The things that one lusts after (passionately feels for), can be a plethora of things. Yes, things of a sexual nature can be lust, but also there is the lust for attention, power, fame, recognition, wealth, etc. We oftentimes fail to recognize our faulty motives, or maybe we do recognize them, but we simply don't care. One pursuing ministry for the sake of self (attention, power, fame, recognition, wealth, etc.) is not operating based on God's standard of ministry.

Earlier I commented that anyone who is "lofty" in His Kingdom is operating in their own kingdom, rather than His. Paul said it like this: "But I do not consider my life of any account as dear to myself, so that I may finish my course and the ministry which I received from the Lord Jesus, to testify solemnly of this Gospel of God's grace" (Acts 20:24 NASB).

He also said, "For to me, to live is Christ and to die is gain" (Philippians 1:21). Meaning, if he were to die, he would gain everything because he would be with Jesus. However, while he yet lived, his life would be all for Him. Paul again said, "For when one person says, 'I am with Paul,' and another, 'I am with Apollos,' are you not ordinary people? What then is Apollos? And what is Paul? Servants through whom you believed, even as the Lord gave opportunity to each one" (I Corinthians 3:4-5 NASB). The person in the ministry means nothing, and the One who anointed the ministry means everything.

Pride

There is much to say about pride, and we will take a moment here to extensively look at this crucial topic. James stated, "…God opposes the proud but gives grace to the humble" (James 4:6). The word "opposes" is "antitasso" and it means "to array as an army; to set oneself in opposition to." This is a very strong word. It is not simply that He dislikes the proud individuals and likes the humble individuals. Rather, He actively fights against and opposes the proud. The question is, why does God so actively oppose such individuals?

The Webster's Dictionary defines pride as, "an unreasonable conceit of one's superiority in talents, beauty, wealth, accomplishments, rank, or elevation in office, which manifests itself in lofty airs, distance, reserve, and often in contempt of others." We see that by simply examining the definition of pride, one can understand why God opposes them to such a degree. These individuals seek to elevate themselves over God. They seek to promote self rather than His Kingdom. Already we see their danger to His Kingdom and His will. Jesus stated, "Whoever is not with me is against me, and whoever does not gather with me scatters" (Matthew 12:30). What He is conveying is that if we do not work in unity with Him, then we work against Him and are His enemy. Not just that, though, if we don't work with Him, according to His will, we will end up scattering instead of gathering. We will drive away instead of pulling close. We will see the opposite results than what was intended. By seeking to promote ourselves and gain our own following, we will instead drive them away, thus losing our following.

God's issue with pride goes far beyond just this. His problem with pride began in heaven with Satan. In Isaiah 14:12-17 and Ezekiel 28:11-19, we are told the backstory of Satan or Lucifer. The story that we see conveyed is one bathed in pride. In Isaiah 14:13 and Ezekiel 28:17, we are told that he became proud due to his beauty, and it corrupted his heart, causing him to think more highly of himself than he ought to. Due to this consuming pride, he thought that he could become as God, propelling himself to an equal, or even greater, position than God. It was this pride that led to his casting out.

This is not the full story though, for then we transition into the Garden of Eden, the story we all know well, the serpent tempting Eve. There is a key line that Satan says to Eve: "But the serpent said to the woman, 'You will not surely die. For God knows that when you eat of it your eyes will be opened, and you will be like God, knowing good and evil'" (Genesis 3:4-5). Notice what finally drew Eve to partake of the fruit? Pride. He tempted her with the idea that caused him to fall, the idea that they could be like God.

It was pride that drove a wedge between God and His beloved creation. It was pride that caused them to have to be cast out from His presence. It was pride that began the whole chain reaction of sin. It is easy to understand why God so strongly stands against pride, for it forever tainted His creation.

John also conveys to us in I John 2:16 that every sin can be summarized into one of three categories, the lust of the flesh, the lust of the eyes, and the pride of life. Therefore,

Kingdom Progression

pride is still one of the driving forces behind the prevalent sin that consumes the world.

Needless to say, pride has no part in the life of one called by God, for it is opposite to His Kingdom. To operate in pride is to operate in the kingdom of darkness which is ruled by Satan. By operating in pride and being in opposition to His will, we, therefore, act in alignment with the will of the enemy.

Humility

Humility, then, is the true way of the Kingdom. Humility is what keeps the minister in alignment with God and His divine will, and it is what drives His Kingdom forward.

We looked at James 4:6 as the starting point in examining why God "opposes the proud," as it says. That Scripture can also be used to examine God's stance toward those who are humble. It says that He "gives grace to the humble." "Grace" is "charis" and it refers to a multitude of things. First off, it refers to a gift freely given, not something earned or deserved. Second, regarding God, it refers to His power working in the individual. This points to several things. One, it refers to the individual walking in the power and authority of God. Two, it refers to the work of God in the life of the individual to bring them further and deeper into Him in relationship.

"Humble" is "tapeinos," and this is a very interesting word, for "tapeinos" can refer to the one who has attained the state of humility before God or one who is undergoing the process of being humbled, which is a very painful process. On the one end, where one is already humble before God, we see a definition along the lines of modesty or a modest assessment of one's self-worth. Meaning, you don't think too highly of yourself because you recognize that everything good about you came from Him anyway (see James 1:17).

The word "tapeinos" can be translated, as "not rising far from the ground." Or in other words, you aren't elevating yourself. These are the individuals to whom God gives grace (in-dwelling power and transformation power). However, as I said, this word can also refer to those who are undergoing the process of being humbled. To those individuals, this word means depressed and oppressed. Why? Because they are feeling the weight of everything on them. And that is the point, it is to crush them. Not so they die, but so they reach a point of recognizing that it isn't all about them, that they can't do it all on their own, and that they do need someone greater than them to lead them. This will not happen until their self-righteous view of themself is utterly destroyed.

There is another wonderful passage that demonstrates the proper stance of humility that we don't often attribute to humility. That is II Corinthians 12:7-10, "So to keep me from becoming conceited because of the surpassing greatness of the revelations, a thorn was given me in the flesh, a messenger of Satan to harass me, to keep me from becoming conceited. Three times I pleaded with the Lord about this, that it should leave me. But he said to me, 'My grace is sufficient for you, for my power is made perfect in weakness.' Therefore I will boast all the more gladly of my weaknesses, so that the power of Christ may rest upon me. For the sake of Christ, then, I am content with weaknesses, insults, hardships, persecutions, and calamities. For when I am weak, then I am strong." We read this and attribute it to a state of physical weakness, circumstantial weakness, or situational weakness. We think this only applies to areas of our lives wherein we are lacking, that in those areas He makes up the difference. However, this is a very conceited mindset (which ironically Paul was stating that God was trying to prevent in Him). Such a mindset states that we can do most things on our own without His help, but in those areas where we just come up short, we know He will come through. This mindset is toxic and is the breeding ground of

Kingdom Progression

pride. Do we forget that Jesus declared, "Apart from me you can do nothing" (John 15:5)? Meaning, we technically dwell in a continual state of weakness, and anything that we do is only because of His strength.

We see that God gave Paul a thorn, but what that thorn is we don't know, and it honestly isn't important. What is important was the purpose of the thorn: to be a constant reminder to Paul that he can't do it on his own. It was to keep him humble. Paul used the wording "weakness." If we pay attention to what Jesus spoke to him, it aligns perfectly with the words of James, "But he said to me, 'My grace is sufficient for you, for my power is made perfect in weakness.' Therefore I will boast all the more gladly of my weaknesses, so that the power of Christ may rest upon me" (II Corinthians 12:9). All of this was for the sole cause of keeping him from becoming conceited, or prideful, boastful, and self-exalted.

Another key passage is I Corinthians 1:27-31, "But God chose what is foolish in the world to shame the wise; God chose what is weak in the world to shame the strong; God chose what is low and despised in the world, even things that are not, to bring to nothing things that are, so that no human being might boast in the presence of God. And because of him you are in Christ Jesus, who became to us wisdom from God, righteousness and sanctification and redemption, so that, as it is written, 'Let the one who boasts, boast in the Lord.'" This passage repeats much of what we have talked about already, but it still bears examination. Paul is conveying to us that God purposely chooses those who, by the world's standards, have no right to even attempt a certain thing. The very idea that they could accomplish certain feats is absurd, and that is the point: because we don't do it of ourselves. The point being, one, "so that no human being might boast in the presence of God." There again we see opposition against the proud, the conceited. God takes active measures to ensure that no one can have even the slightest opportunity to be such. Two, so that any boasting that is had is given to the Lord: ensuring that He receives all the praise, glory, and honor for all that is done because it is Him doing it anyway. We are simply His vessels by which He does it.

We will examine the Gifts of the Spirit and the Five-Fold Ministry in-depth in subsequent chapters, but one key aspect of both is that they are entirely from Him.

> Now there are varieties of gifts, but the same Spirit; and there are varieties of service, but the same Lord; and there are varieties of activities, but it is the same God who empowers them all in everyone.
> -I Corinthians 12:4-6

> And He gave the apostles, the prophets, the evangelists, the shepherds and teachers.
> -Ephesians 4:11

The keys in these two passages being that it is His Spirit that empowers every gift, and it is He who gives or appoints individuals to different Offices.

There is also a key parable given by Jesus that ought to be examined when speaking on humility, for it conveys another crucial aspect of humility that is often overlooked. In Luke 14:7-11, Jesus paints the picture of a wedding feast. At the said feast, He conveys that when you go to take your seat, do not assume that you ought to sit in a place of honor. Instead, you are a guest, not the Master of the feast, so who are you to judge the level of honor of which you dwell in? For if you pridefully sit in a place of honor, another will likely come that is more honored than you, and the Master will ask you to move. Rather, assume a place of lowly honor so when the Master arrives, if you are to be placed in greater honor, He can elevate you. Is it not better to be elevated than humiliated? Unfortunately, we fail so often to operate in this place. For we walk into the room and, because our name is

Kingdom Progression

known and widely recognized, we automatically think that we own the place. We are to be highly honored. Remember, your name doesn't matter. The only name that matters is His Name. The Name above every other name, as Paul stated in Philippians 2:9.

When we walk into a room, rather than assuming that we deserve to be honored, assume a place and position of servanthood.

What Ministry is

What does it mean to operate in ministry?

Looking back to a passage quoted when talking about what ministry is not, Paul said, "For when one person says, 'I am with Paul,' and another, 'I am with Apollos,' are you not ordinary people? What then is Apollos? And what is Paul? Servants through whom you believed, even as the Lord gave opportunity to each one" (I Corinthians 3:4-5 NASB). Paul followed that Scripture with, "I planted, Apollos watered, but God gave the growth. So neither he who plants nor he who waters is anything, but only God who gives the growth. He who plants and he who waters are one, and each will receive his wages according to his labor. For we are God's fellow workers. You are God's field, God's building" (I Corinthians 3:6-9). Paul also declared, "For to me, to live is Christ and to die is gain" (Philippians 1:21).

Servanthood

First, we see that within the Corinthian Church, sects had been forming wherein the different ministers of the Gospel were being glorified. Two such individuals that were being glorified were Paul and Apollos. Paul sought to emphatically shut this argument down. First, he described himself and Apollos as "ordinary people." This is one word in Greek, "sarkikos." This word focuses on the carnality of humanity, emphasizing how we are but nothing when compared to Divinity (God). He sought to first tear down the false idea that ministers were something mystical, or incredibly special: maybe even sort of like demigods. Some names (Apollos, Paul, Peter) had been elevated to a position where they were worshipped and honored as the ones that saved them. Paul, then, emphasized that they were merely human, carnal, and ordinary. He was putting himself, Peter, and Apollos on the same plain as the rest of the Corinthian Church. He then went to an even greater extent and defined them as "servants." This is "diakonos" which means, "one who executes the commands of their master; a servant to a king." Peter, in his second epistle, expounded upon this idea. He begins his letter with, "Simon Peter, a servant and apostle of Jesus Christ..." (II Peter 1:1). "Servant" here is a different word than the one used by Paul, "diakonos." The word used by Peter emphasizes the idea of servanthood to an even greater degree. This word is "doulos," and it means "a slave; a bondman." Interestingly enough, when we hear "slave," we think of one forced into slavery. However, this word, "doulos," can also refer to one who willingly subjected themselves to the will of another, therefore, not forced slavery, but willing slavery. It implies such a great love that drives the individual to want to do anything and everything that their master desires.

  Then Paul makes the statement that it wasn't just that they willingly subjected themselves to Christ, but that He also "gave opportunity." This is the Greek word "didōmi." "Didōmi" is an extremely rich word with its meaning reaching far and wide. Embedded within the idea of all its different definitions is the idea of being anointed. We will come back to this, for it deserves considerable examination. First, let's finish examining our quoted passages.

Kingdom Progression

Unity

Paul continues his discourse by focusing on his and Apollos' ministry, stating how he (Paul) planted and Apollos watered, but that it was ultimately God that gave the growth. Here is another key aspect of ministry: unity. A very common mentality and attitude in many ministers today is that they think they have to do everything alone. That mentality may come from a place of pride and arrogance, thinking that they can do it better than anyone else. Or it may come from a place of ignorance, not realizing that others around them are meant to help them. Either way, such a mentality will destroy a seed. When we consider the words of Paul, note that his calling was to plant: to speak the Word of God (plant the seed) to the hearts of men (the soil). If you look at the Book of Acts, you see that Paul was constantly on the move. Planting seed in a city but then moving to the next city, oftentimes rather quickly. Planting a seed there, and then moving again, etc. Very seldom do we see Paul abiding in one place for an extended time. This is why Apollos, then, came along behind Paul: he was not trying to undo the work of Paul but expound upon such. He sought to nurture the Word that Paul had planted previously.

Another false mentality and attitude many ministers have is, "Well I can do it better than they did." It's not about who does it better, but it is about operating in the gifting that He has given to you. Apollos came along behind (but also beside) Paul and watered what he had planted. They each played a differing role in the development of the seed. Again, this goes back to unity. First, we must know our place in the process. Do you plant? Do you water? Do you reap the harvest? What role do you play? Second, we cannot work in opposition to those that came before us and those who will come after us. We must recognize that we are all unified in the Body of Christ and are called for His purpose and will. We don't serve our means, rather, His means.

Kristopher David Grepke

Unity is key to the proper operation of the Kingdom of God. So Paul wrote, "I appeal to you, brothers, by the name of our Lord Jesus Christ, that all of you agree, and that there be no divisions among you, but that you be united in the same mind and the same judgment" (I Corinthians 1:10). Likewise, Peter wrote, "Finally, all of you, have unity of mind, sympathy, brotherly love, a tender heart, and a humble mind" (I Peter 3:8). There is a plethora of other Scriptures that also convey the essentiality of unity in the Church of Christ (see Philippians 2:2; Colossians 3:14; Romans 12:16 as a few examples). One crucial thing to understand about unity is that God will only dwell where it is present, He will not dwell amidst disunity or discord.

In Matthew 12:22-32 Jesus is speaking to the people about how a divided kingdom cannot stand. When there is disunity and discord and infighting, there will be the destruction of that kingdom. He spoke this because the religious rulers were thinking in their hearts that He was casting out demons by Beelzebub (another name for Satan). He thwarted this by drawing attention to the fact that it made no sense. Since Jesus focused intently on the essentiality of the kingdom that is not divided but unified, what should we surmise regarding how He desires His Kingdom to operate?

Also, look to the Book of Acts for further demonstration of this truth. In Acts 2:1-4 we see the official birth of His Kingdom on earth, His Church being born (the outpouring of His Spirit). Notice in this passage that this did not transpire until they were all "in one accord" (Acts 2:1 KJV). This phrase is one Greek word, "homothumadon," and it means "with one mind; with one passion." Meaning, they had laid aside their ideas, their agendas, and their plans and had come into such unity that they all shared the same vision and heartfelt desire.

There is a well-known passage on unity we all quote: "Behold, how good and pleasant it is when brothers dwell in unity" (Psalms 133:1). This is where we stop, and it's a shame we do so, for the following two verses are crucial: "It is like the precious oil on the head, running down on the beard, on the beard of Aaron, running down on the collar of his robes! It is like the dew of Hermon, which falls on the mountains of Zion! For there the LORD has commanded the blessing, life forevermore" (Psalms 133:2-3). The word "ointment" in Hebrew is "shemen," and it refers to the anointing oil. Therefore, we see very clearly that unity is integral to anointing. Again, we will come back to anointing and thoroughly break it down, for it is integral that one understands the anointing if they are to understand the call of God.

A key aspect of unity in ministry is not just unity amongst fellow ministers, but it includes unity with God. Once again, look back to the words of Paul, when he stated how he and Apollos worked together to plant and water (as we have discussed), but then he notes that it was God who expressly gave the growth. This is pointing to the fact that just because he planted and Apollos watered doesn't mean that they caused anything to grow. He says that "neither he who plants nor he who waters is anything." The vital thing to understand here is that the only reason God gave the growth is because they were working according to His Will.

Paul said, "For as many as are led by the Spirit of God, they are the sons of God" (Romans 8:14). The word "led" here is "agō" and it means "to lead by taking hold of." Meaning, we are led by the Spirit when the Spirit has fully and completely taken hold of us. Meaning, it is when we have laid aside ourselves and given ourselves over completely to Him and His Will. When He directs us to minister to people we aren't comfortable with, or in a place where we aren't sure how they'll respond, we don't make excuses as to why we can't minister, or try and point out a better place in which to minister. It is crucial to remember that it is not your ministry. It is not subjected to you; it does not follow you. It is subjected to the One who gave it, which is Christ. We are truly only His ministers when we are subjected to His will. Saying what He wants to say, going where He wants to go, and doing what He wants to do.

Reap What is Sowed

Paul also states that "each will receive his wages according to his labor." Now, we think of this as, "As long as I'm working, God will bless me." However, this isn't the correct train of thought. This word "wages" is "misthos," and it does not strictly refer to the payment one receives after completing a job. It refers, rather, to whatever the individual deserves, whether that be blessing or cursing, reward or punishment. What the individual receives is strictly determined by their labor. Now again, the quality of labor is not determined by the individual completing the work; rather, it is determined by the one who hired them. In this case, it is God, for it is He who calls every minister to His work.

What we see, then, is that to be rewarded with a blessing, we must work according to His standard, which is His divine will. If we are not subjecting ourselves to His will, but instead operating out of our own, we run the risk of bringing cursing and punishment upon ourselves.

There is one last Scripture I want to look at before moving on to the anointing: Philippians 1:21, "For to me to live is Christ, and to die is gain." This is one of my favorite passages of Scripture, and I quote it very often. A prayer I often pray is that God would help me to reach a place where I could truthfully and confidently echo these words of Paul, for they are such powerful yet simple words.

First, we see that Paul declared that for him, to "live" is Christ. "Live" here is "zaō" and it is a very wide-ranging word. It encompasses every aspect of what the word "life" could refer to, that is, both the physical aspect of life and the spiritual aspect of life: living in this life and in the life to come. What Paul was conveying here is that everything that he was, none of it was for himself, but all that pertained to him was totally and completely bathed and saturated in Christ. Then, he states that "to die is gain." Was Paul suicidal? Not by any means. Here is what Paul was conveying to us: he was stating that while he yet lived, all that he was and ever would be was completely and totally for Him. But when he died, he would gain it all. Why? How? Because he lived so completely and totally for Him, when he died, he would gain Christ. Paul had such confidence in this because he lived intentionally. We looked at this Scripture previously, but we needed to do so here as well due to how it coincided with our discussion.

The Anointing

Talent vs Anointing

Understanding anointing is truly vital when speaking on the call of God toward individuals into ministry. Everything rests upon the anointing. Anointing is often misconstrued with talent or natural ability. For example, someone sings well on the praise team and so it is naturally thought that they are anointed. This is not necessarily true, for talent does not equate to anointing. Likewise, someone may be a talented speaker, but this does not mean that they are anointed by God to speak.

I think that it would be helpful if we started by examining talent, or natural gifting, because as I said, we misconstrue talent for anointing. What is talent? Well, as stated, it is something naturally possessed by the individual. They may have had to work to refine that skill, but they were born with the natural inclination for that skill. The Webster's Dictionary and Oxford Languages agree with this assessment of talent. Now this is not to say that the talent you were naturally born with is pointless and worthless. For as stated previously when speaking on the question, Can God Trust You?, I stated how one should be actively finding ways in which they can serve the church beyond their unique gifting. Meaning, God has given us all different gifts, and as the Parable of the Talents demonstrates, we have a duty to use those talents in a manner that furthers His Kingdom. If we waste what He has given us in the world, then what we have will be taken away (see Matthew 25:14-30). We should take what we have been given and use it faithfully for Him. Again, this is not the same as anointing, it is merely making your gifing available to Christ..

Looking back to our passage in which we defined what a minister was, Paul said, "Servants through whom you believed, even as the Lord gave opportunity to each one" (I Corinthians 3:5 NASB). The key here is that Paul said, "The Lord gave opportunity." This "gave opportunity" here is, "didōmi," which refers to the anointing. Meaning, the ministry that Paul and Apollos operated in transcended their natural abilities and tapped into something that distinctly came from God. We are going to look at the Gifts of the Spirit and the Five-Fold Ministry in the latter chapters, but I've pointed out before how every gift and office were distinctly given by God (see I Corinthians 12:4-6; Ephesians 4:11 as the two previous examples given).

We have also previously looked at I Corinthians 1:27-31: "But God chose what is foolish in the world to shame the wise; God chose what is weak in the world to shame the strong; God chose what is low and despised in the world, even things that are not, to bring to nothing things that are, so that no human being might boast in the presence of God. And because of him you are in Christ Jesus, who became to us wisdom from God, righteousness and sanctification and redemption, so that, as it is written, 'Let the one who boasts, boast in the Lord.'" Again, God wants us to use our unique talents for the betterment of His Body. This passage is not saying to not use what talent He has given you. What

Kingdom Progression

this passage is conveying is that for His distinct work, as an example, He chose those who can't naturally speak well to speak, and those who aren't natural leaders to lead. All of this emphatically conveys to us that the anointing transcends talent.

Cultivating the Anointing

Therefore, we are brought back to the question, "What is the anointing?" This is a multifaceted question that will take some time to answer, which is why I left space for it here at the end of this chapter.

Paul said, "And it is God who establishes us with you in Christ, and has anointed us, and who has also put his seal on us and given us his Spirit in our hearts as a guarantee" (II Corinthians 1:21-22). To truly understand what it means to be anointed by God, we must first go back to the Old Testament to discover its origin and its purpose. The understanding we possess of it today is birthed from what was conveyed to us in the Old Testament.

> The LORD said to Moses, "Take the finest spices: of liquid myrrh 500 shekels, and of sweet-smelling cinnamon half as much, that is, 250, and 250 of aromatic cane, and 500 of cassia, according to the shekel of the sanctuary, and a hin of olive oil. And you shall make of these a sacred anointing oil blended as by the perfumer; it shall be a holy anointing oil. With it you shall anoint the tent of meeting and the ark of the testimony, and the table and all its utensils, and the lampstand and its utensils, and the altar of incense, and the altar of burnt offering with all its utensils and the basin and its stand. You shall consecrate them, that they may be most

> holy. Whatever touches them will become holy. You shall anoint Aaron and his sons, and consecrate them, that they may serve me as priests. And you shall say to the people of Israel, 'This shall be my holy anointing oil throughout your generations.
> -Exodus 30:22-31

Contained in this passage are the ingredients of the anointing oil and the purpose thereof. It is integral that we break this down and fully grasp this if we are to understand the anointing.

First, we see that what the anointing oil is comprised of is "the finest spices." This word, "finest," is "rô'sh," and it does not simply refer to the best or the most valuable, rather, it refers to that which is above: that which sits above the rest. It refers to something that is the head, or chief, over others. It is not simply that these ingredients are the most expensive, but that they are the best quality, they put all others to shame, and they sit high above all others. Already we see that what makes up the anointing is not ordinary, normal, average, and so on. Rather, what it is made up of is only the best, only that which has been proven, only that which has demonstrated time and time again that it sits high above all else.

From the very start we are again directed to this truth of the question, Can God Trust You? How faithful are you? How devoted are you? How obedient are you? How submitted are you? How consistent are you? We see emphatically that the answer to these questions determines the anointing.

The first ingredient we see is myrrh. Myrrh is an extremely interesting ingredient, for myrrh is very bitter. This may seem odd. Why would God include bitterness in the anointing? The key to understanding this is a proper examination of the process of acquiring myrrh and the process by which you add it to other products. Myrrh comes from a tree with a very complicated name, Commiphora Myrrha. The only way to extract myrrh from this tree is to wound it. To cut it. Therefore, we see that the wounding exposes bitterness. It does not stop here. For then you harvest the myrrh, and it comes out waxy, sort of like gum, which then hardens. After it hardens, to add it to a mixture, you must crush it into a powder. We see, then, that the first ingredient of the anointing is for one to be wounded as to expose the bitterness within and then for that bitterness to be crushed.

Cinnamon is the next ingredient we see. Cinnamon today may be regarded as a commonality, but in times past it was a major delicacy. It was mainly prized for its sweet aroma and the flavor that enhanced whatever it was placed in. It had other uses as well, such as in the process of embalming mummies in Ancient Egypt, but its primary use was for its aroma and taste. In essence, it made everything better. Again, when we come to the process by which the cinnamon was added into mixtures such as the anointing oil, it had to be crushed and ground into fine powder.

Third was the calamus plant. Calamus also had a very sweet aroma, much like cinnamon. However, there is a distinct difference between calamus and cinnamon in that calamus is potentially toxic if ingested. The image this paints for us is one of hypocrisy. Here we have something that gives the presentation of being sweet, but in actuality it can be deadly. Jesus gave a stark warning against hypocrisy (see Luke 12:1-3). Even the smallest bit of hypocrisy is like leaven, it will overtake the whole. Again, we see that the process in which it is added into a mixture is to be crushed. Any amount of hypocrisy within us must be thoroughly crushed.

The fourth ingredient, Cassia, is related to cinnamon and is extremely similar to such. They share a similar smell and taste with cassia being slightly thicker. Cassia is also used in the same capacities as cinnamon. Once again, it must be crushed and ground.

This brings us to the final ingredient of the anointing oil, which is, olive oil. Olive oil was the base liquid into which all the other ground-up ingredients were added. Altogether this mixture exuded such an overwhelming aroma, with each of the different spices, and the olive oil itself, possessing such strong smells. You couldn't walk into a room without being overwhelmed by the aroma thereof. It would consume all your senses. There was no way that you wouldn't notice and give heed to the overwhelming aroma of the anointing. We get excited about this because that tells us that when we are anointed, people can't help but notice, for the anointing will exude from us. It will captivate every sense of those who are in our presence. In our carnality, we want to revel in such. Before you begin to revel, let me remind you that the first five ingredients had to be crushed, and secondly, we need to understand the process in which the olive oil, the final ingredient, was made.

Olive oil is made by what is called an olive press. Its action quite literally aligns with the name. Its sole purpose is to press and crush the olives until their juice runs out. Therefore, we see a common theme across every ingredient of the anointing, it has to be crushed. Not just that, for as we have seen, not every ingredient that made up the anointing was all good or all bad. There was a balance between the two. What this tells us, then, is that it's not just the bad aspects of us that need to be thoroughly crushed, but also the good aspects of us. Every fiber of our being has to be thoroughly and completely crushed before the anointing can come.

Purpose of the Anointing

The reason for this severe amount of crushing is conveyed also in our quoted passage of Scripture. The purpose of this anointing oil was to consecrate unto God. The word "consecrate" is "qâdash," and it means "to consecrate, sanctify, prepare, dedicate, be hallowed, be holy,

Kingdom Progression

be sanctified, be separate." The key to all this is that we are separated unto God, for His divine purpose. The entire purpose for the crushing of all that makes up who we are is so that we will be entirely and completely separated unto Him to be used for His purpose. We must first be crushed so that we are removed from the equation. It isn't about you. When we are anointed, we are set apart unto Him. Our lives are completely devoted to Him. As Paul said so beautifully (quoting it once again), "For to me to live is Christ, and to die is gain" (Philippians 1:21).

Looking back for a moment to a previously quoted passage, Psalms 133:2, we see the coverage of anointing, for it says, "It is like the precious oil on the head, running down on the beard, on the beard of Aaron, running down on the collar of his robes!" The anointing oil always began at the head, the top, of the individual. However, it did not stop at the head, it was allowed to flow freely where it covered the entirety of the individual. The process of anointing in your life has not been completed until it covers the entirety of who you are, from head to feet. This falls in line with what we have discussed, all that you are must be crushed before you can be anointed, for the anointing is meant to cover every part of you. The reason for it being so important that all of you is covered under the anointing is that God can only use you to the full extent that He desires if you have been fully anointed. Meaning, if the anointing has covered your head (mind) but not your hands, He cannot work through you in how He desires. Or if it covers your mouth, but not your feet, He cannot move through you how He desires.

One True Anointing

Looking back one last time to Exodus, after God gives the ingredients for the anointing oil and what it is to be used on, He then conveys to Moses another key aspect of the anointing. The LORD said to Moses, "It shall not be poured on the body of an ordinary person, and you shall make no other like it in composition. It is holy, and it shall be holy to you" (Exodus 30:22). Following this, God told Moses that anyone that misused the anointing would be "cut off from his people" (v.23). What God is conveying to Moses here is absolutely crucial. One, He states that not just anyone can be anointed. The anointing is not something that is just irresponsibly poured out onto whoever would so desire it. Rather, the anointing is reserved for those who have been found worthy in the sight of God to be anointed. What does this entail? The answer to that would be all that we have discussed. This takes us back, once again, to the question, Can God Trust You? In addition, it points to the process of the anointing oil being made by crushing. Only those who have been deemed trustworthy by God and have endured the process of the crushing may be anointed.

He also conveys to Moses another key aspect, that is, to not manufacture a fake anointing, a mimic anointing. Don't try and create something that looks similar to the anointing of God to exalt yourself to a position you are not worthy of. You either have it, or you don't. To try and fake the anointing is to judge yourself as worthy of banishment from the people of God. We must be careful to ensure that we are walking in accordance with the will of God and His Kingdom and not according to ourselves, lest we bring about our exile.

This is our base of understanding the anointing. There is still more we must unpack, for it is all vital for us to understand, for the anointing is inseparable from true, called-of-God ministry.

The Continual Process

The next aspect of anointing we must understand is displayed through the earthly ministry of Jesus. Our focus is actually on the latter end of His life, specifically, His time in

Kingdom Progression

the Garden of Gethsemane. What we often don't realize, but that Luke made more plain in his Gospel account, was that the Garden of Gethsemane was located on the Mount of Olives and was specifically a place where an olive press resided. Jesus went to the place of crushing at the most integral and significant point of His life, the moments leading up to His crucifixion. What we must understand about Jesus' visit here is that He did not come just at this moment in time. His mentality was not, "Oh, well, it's about that time, better start getting ready." The Gospel of Luke says, "And he came out and went, as was his custom, to the Mount of Olives, and the disciples followed him" (Luke 22:39). The word "custom" is "ethos," and it also means, "habit." Meaning, coming to the place of crushing was something He did regularly. If the place in which He went was His habit, it is safe to surmise that the prayer He prayed was also His habit, "nevertheless, not my will, but yours, be done" (Luke 22:42).

What we learn from the life of Jesus is that the process of anointing is not something that happens just once; rather, it is something that happens again, and again, and again. Why? Because part of the crushing process is submitting to His will and forsaking your own. It is not possible that this could only be a one-time thing, we must submit daily. If you've only been crushed once but never again, it means you've never revisited the place of crushing, and thus you have abandoned His will in favor of your own.

The Anointing that Transforms

Another thing to understand about the anointing is demonstrated for us in the life of David. God called Samuel to anoint David to be the next king of Israel, for Saul had forsaken and abandoned the will of God (going back to if you try and create your own anointing, you will be forced out). "Then Samuel took the horn of oil and anointed him in the midst of his brothers. And the Spirit of the LORD rushed upon David from that day forward. And Samuel rose up and went to Ramah. Now the Spirit of the LORD departed from Saul, and a harmful spirit from the LORD tormented him" (I Samuel 16:13-14). David was now anointed, and we see the effects of this anointing immediately in his life. When Saul was seeking one to play for him to soothe his anxiety, this is what one of his servants said, "Behold, I have seen a son of Jesse the Bethlehemite, who is skillful in playing, a man of valor, a man of war, prudent in speech, and a man of good presence, and the LORD is with him" (I Samuel 16:18). There was no reason for this servant to think so highly of David, for even his own family (before he was anointed) thought so little of him as to not have him stand before the Prophet (see I Samuel 16:11). The only reason that we can reasonably come to as to why this servant gave such an impressive report about David to Saul was due to the anointing. As stated previously, the anointing carries such a strong and overwhelming aroma that its presence absolutely cannot be denied.

Waiting in the Anointing

There is much that the life of David conveys to us about the anointing that is crucial to understand. For, again, we get excited about the idea of being noticed by others because we are drawn to pride and arrogance, and self-promotion. However, I ask you, did David immediately become king of Israel after being anointed? No. Most scholars agree that David had to wait fourteen to fifteen years after the anointing by Samuel before he became king. That is a long wait. Here I pose a question to you: can you wait for the proper process of anointing? Or are you impatient and trying to rush God?

The Bible says very often that we are to wait on the Lord (see Psalms 37:9; 52:9; 123:2; 130:5; Proverbs 20:22 and many more). We are also told by Solomon, "For everything there is a season, and a time for every matter

Kingdom Progression

under heaven" (Ecclesiastes 3:1). Meaning, God has a perfect will and purposeful time for everything that is to happen. In our pride and arrogance, we think that we know better than God: that He doesn't see it as we do, and He just doesn't understand our situation, and so we think this one particular path is better than the one He laid out. This train of thought is utter foolishness, for we are told that "his understanding is beyond measure" (Psalms 147:5). Then the Apostle John took it one step further than that and declared that "He knows everything" (I John 3:20). The only reason we think that God doesn't understand is that we don't realize how personal of a God He is. Furthermore, we don't realize how personal of a God He is because we do not know Him personally.

We see clearly that we are admonished to wait on God, that He has a divine time for all matters, and that He knows best because He sees and knows all. Beyond even these things, we are told that one of the Fruit of the Spirit is patience (see Galatians 5:22). Embedded in the idea of biblical patience (makrothumia in Greek) is the concept of submission or surrender. True patience is only achieved when one concedes that they do not know all, or do not know best, and even if they don't fully understand what He is doing or why, they willingly submit to His divine will and plan. Patience is giving God the time and space to do His work in our lives.

Going back to David, he had to wait fourteen to fifteen years until the fulfillment of what Samuel had spoken over him. David was not perfect; rather, he was human: living in a day and age apart from Christ's in-dwelling Spirit. I am sure there were days, months, maybe even years where he was edging on impatience and just wanting to do things his way. Nevertheless, through it all, David waited on the perfect timing of God. Patience is key to the anointing.

One reason why David had to wait so long was that God had to prepare him for the position he was going to be operating in. Before the anointing, all David knew was shepherding, but God had called him to be a king. The positional difference between a shepherd and a king is vast. I am sure that David's experience as a shepherd helped him greatly, for his sole duty was the watchful care of the flock, and this is a similar role of the king. However, there is a big difference between caring for a few sheep and caring for thousands of human beings. Needless to say, God had to prepare David for the role of the king.

Here is another aspect of the anointing back then: the crushing is not the only process involved in the anointing. Just because you are anointed does not mean you are automatically ready for every position He has for you. One thing that my Pastor says is, "God will not give you shoes too big for your feet," implying that God will not give you something that you have not grown to a point wherein you can fill such. Just because He has anointed you does not mean you are finished and ready, God still has to prepare you for what He has in store. This will be a lengthy process. For you may grow enough to fill a certain position here, so God directs you there, but that is not what He ultimately has for you. Therefore, while you abide in that position, He continues to grow you. Then you reach a point in your growth where you can now fill this position, so He moves you there, and so on. It is crucial to understand that we cannot become complacent simply because He has anointed us. We must surrender to His timing and be patient and allow Him to grow us so that we can fulfill what He has called us to.

Honor the Anointing

We also see, continuing with the life of David, another key aspect of the anointing. We all know how the story goes: Saul came to realize that the anointing now rested upon David, but instead of walking in humility and working

Kingdom Progression

to prepare David, he sought to kill him. David, responding how we all would, ran for his life. During this time of hide and seek, we read of two important occurrences.

If we look at I Samuel 24 and 26 we read of two instances where Saul and his company were resting, and during the night David snuck in and had the opportunity to kill Saul. However, both times he turned aside. Talking to Saul, David said, "Behold, this day your eyes have seen how the LORD gave you today into my hand in the cave. And some told me to kill you, but I spared you. I said, 'I will not put out my hand against my lord, for he is the LORD'S anointed'" (I Samuel 24:10). What is interesting is that we were told that when David was anointed, God's Spirit left Saul, and an evil spirit filled the void (see I Samuel 16:14). Therefore, Saul was no longer anointed. The anointing had left Saul, yet David still honored him as anointed because he had not yet been promoted to the position of king.

We also read in II Samuel 1 of David hearing of Saul and Jonathan's deaths. One would think that David would be jumping for joy. For not only was his pursuer now dead, but the kingship was now his. Regardless, this is not what we see. Instead, he mourned Saul's death. We realize this when we see a young man who escaped the battle and ran to find David to tell him the news. As he relays to David the events, we discover that he (the young man) killed Saul at his request. David's response was, "How is it you were not afraid to put out your hand to destroy the LORD'S anointed" (II Samuel 1:14)? Then he had the young man executed for the act he committed against Saul. We also see that David passionately wept and mourned and fasted over the death of Saul.

Why? Should not David be rejoicing? No, because David understood the principle of honor. Honor is crucial to anointing. There may be times in your walk in God's gifting that you have to wait on those who came before you to move before you can also move up. It is important that in these times we give honor to those who came before us. We cannot seek to overthrow them so that we can have their position. We must honor the anointed of God. Honor also flows in the opposite direction. Saul did not operate in honor, but if he had, he would've brought David up and worked with him to prepare him. When we see God preparing another to one day operate where He has us, we absolutely cannot operate in the mentality of, "No! This is my ministry! You can't have it!" Remember, it's not your ministry, it's His! If He desires to give it to another, we must humbly submit to His will and give honor to those who are coming behind us.

Romans 12:9-21 is a critical passage, the ESV gives this passage the subtitle "Marks of a True Christian." Much of what Paul writes about comes alongside what we have said here on honor. It is a lengthy passage, but it is important we truly walk in all that Paul conveyed.

> Let love be genuine. Abhor what is evil; hold fast to what is good. Love one another with brotherly affection. Outdo one another in showing honor. Do not be slothful in zeal, be fervent in spirit, serve the Lord. Rejoice in hope, be patient in tribulation, be constant in prayer. Contribute to the needs of the saints and seek to show hospitality. Bless those who persecute you; bless and do not curse them. Rejoice with those who rejoice, weep with those who weep. Live in harmony with one another. Do not be haughty, but associate with the lowly. Never be wise in your own sight. Repay no one evil for evil, but give thought to do what is honorable in the sight of all. If possible, so far as it depends on you, live peaceably with all. Beloved, never avenge yourselves, but leave it to the wrath of God, for it is written, "Vengeance is mine,

Kingdom Progression

> I will repay, says the Lord." To the contrary, "if your enemy is hungry, feed him; if he is thirsty, give him something to drink; for by so doing you will heap burning coals on his head." Do not be overcome by evil, but overcome evil with good.
> -Romans 12:9-21

Promotion Follows Anointing

There is one last thing to look at from the life of David regarding the anointing. We have, in a very simple manner, summarized the life of David during his process of becoming king of Israel. We have seen how he did not immediately become king after being anointed but had to wait fourteen to fifteen years for the fulfillment thereof. We also have seen how there was a process that followed the anointing that prepared him for the office he was soon to fill. Last, but certainly not least, we have seen how throughout his whole experience, honor was his motto. He constantly and consistently gave honor to a man who did not deserve it. Why? Because by honoring Saul, he was honoring the position he filled, and by honoring the position he filled, he honored the God who brought about that position. David's honor toward Saul was never because of Saul (as Saul did much evil), but it was because David honored God.

Here we arrive at the final part of David's story that we will look at. Saul and Jonathan are now dead, so a young man brings the news to David, along with the crown and armlet of the king as proof. Did David then become king? No. David did not take the crown and place it on his head and dance around saying, "Look at me, I'm the king!" No. The first thing David did was seek the face of God.

> After this David inquired of the LORD, "Shall I go up into any of the cities of Judah?" And

> the LORD said to him, "Go up." David said, "To which shall I go up?" And he said, "To Hebron."
> -II Samuel 2:1

David obeys the voice of God and goes where He commanded him to go. However, David did not go there as a self-declared king. Rather, David went to Hebron (which is in Judah) in humility. He did not usurp the throne; rather, it was the people of Judah who then anointed David king over Judah (see II Samuel 2:4). The story does not end there, for we see a divide transpire that caused Israel to anoint its king (Ish-Bosheth, son of Saul). Fast-forwarding to II Samuel chapter five, we see that David had to wait seven and a half years before being anointed king over all of Israel. When he was finally anointed, it was the elders (the leaders) of Israel that anointed him (see II Samuel 5:3).

Here is what we see from examining this chapter of David's life: just because you're anointed and a position opens up, it does not give you the authority to promote yourself to that position. David was first anointed by God, and then that anointing was recognized by the people, and they came into agreement with God and also anointed David. You may have to wait, but you must submit to the authority of your church leaders. If they are seeking the will of God and you are truly anointed, they will come to recognize the anointing on your life and promote you. However, if you try and promote yourself, it will only end in the destruction of the ministry and the removal of the anointing on your life. We must practice patience and humility amid the process of the anointing. We must wait for those above us to recognize what God has placed on us. When they do, they will then open the door unto us to walk through.

The Flow of the Anointing

Kingdom Progression

One final thought on the anointing: we must understand how we are to flow with the anointing. It is vital to remember that the anointing is of God, not of yourself. Therefore, the anointing is in accordance with the will and plan of God, not your own. It flows with His character and design. Therefore, what is the flow of the anointing?

II Kings 4:1-7 conveys to us a story we all know well: the story of Elisha and the widow who owed a great debt she could not pay. What we need to understand from this story was what transpired with the oil. Elisha told the widow to go and borrow all the empty vessels she could find and then to take what little oil she had and pour it into every empty vessel she was able to gather up. The story goes that she and her son began to pour out the oil, and what was once a minuscule amount of oil began to fill all these empty vessels. The oil only stopped flowing when they stopped pouring it into empty vessels.

Here is what we see: the anointing is not meant to be confined inside you but is meant to be poured out. The longer it stays imprisoned within you, the less and less you will begin to have. The only way to keep the flow of anointing in your life is constantly pouring it out into empty vessels.

Look to the words of Paul, quoting Jesus, "In all things I have shown you that by working hard in this way we must help the weak and remember the words of the Lord Jesus, how he himself said, 'It is more blessed to give than to receive'" (Acts 20:35). Jesus Himself said, "Give, and it will be given to you. Good measure, pressed down, shaken together, running over, will be put into your lap. For with the measure you use it will be measured back to you" (Luke 6:38). Looking once more to the words of Paul: "Do not be deceived: God is not mocked, for whatever one sows, that will he also reap" (Galatians 6:7).

One of the most fundamental laws of the Kingdom of God is to give. Do not hoard the things that God has blessed you with. Do not store them up or hide them in jars in your closet. Take what He has given you and pour it out. You may think that if you pour it out that you will lose what He has given you. If so, you do not understand God, for God does not operate in compliance with the natural order. He created the natural order, so He can therefore transcend it. The only way to get more in the Kingdom of God is to give more. If you selfishly hold onto what He has given unto you, He will take even that away from you.

Conclusion

Much has been examined here, particularly regarding the anointing. We must understand this, for this is what it truly means to be called of God: that His anointing rests upon you.

We cannot operate according to our ideas or standards. We must walk in submission to His will, for it is His calling, it is His ministry, it is His anointing, and we are simply stewards thereof. We must displace all pride and arrogance from us and walk in humility. We cannot forsake the process that He has determined to prepare us for the anointing and the ministry. We must allow Him to do in us and through us what He needs to do. We must walk in patience and humility and honor.

Finally, we cannot hoard what He has given, thinking that it is owed to us and is now our possession. It may be in your hands but only because He placed it there. He did not place it in your hands to hold onto it but to let it flow. We must freely pour out what He has given, and only then will we be given more.

God has called us all to ministry, no matter what that may look like. Whether it is speaking behind the pulpit in some capacity, singing, children's ministry, cleaning, and so on. Every ministry is crucial to the proper function of the body of Christ, even if a ministry is not in the limelight (see I Corinthians 12:22-26). No matter the ministry, even if it isn't

Kingdom Progression

people-facing, we still must operate properly in accordance with His Word and standard. Furthermore, if one only feels called to clean the church, there is still an anointing for such. Therefore, even in the seemingly insignificant ministries (though there is no such thing) we must understand His anointing.

4
The Spiritual Gifts

Only now, after we have discussed His Kingdom (how one enters and abides therein), what He looks at to determine if He can trust an individual to operate in ministry, and what ministry is and the anointing behind it, can we begin to delve into the spiritual Gifts and the Five-Fold Ministry. We have such a high view of these things and want so badly to operate in them and to be called into the Five-Fold Ministry, and that is wonderful. We ought to have such a zeal for the promises of God. However, we cannot forsake what comes before the Gifts and the Five-Fold Ministry, or else we will never attain those promises. We must balance our zeal for the gifts of God with proper alignment with His process of promotion.

Finding Your Place

Before delving into this topic, we ought to discuss that it is important that we find our place in the church. We touched on this briefly when speaking on devotion to the Church, but we will examine it more thoroughly here.

In I Corinthians 12:12-21 Paul gives the analogy of the Church as a human body: "For just as the body is one and has many members, and all the members of the body, though many, are one body, so it is with Christ. For in one Spirit, we were all baptized into one body—Jews or Greeks, slaves or free—and all were made to drink of one Spirit. For the body does not consist of one member but of many. If the foot should say, 'Because I am not a hand, I do not belong to the body,' that would not make it any less a part of the body. And if the ear should say, 'Because I am not an eye, I do not belong to the body,' that would not make it any less a part of the body. If the whole body were an eye, where would be the sense of hearing? If the whole body were an ear, where would be the sense of smell? But as it is, God arranged the members in the body, each one of them, as he chose. If all were a single member, where would the body be? As it is, there are many parts, yet one body. The eye cannot say to the hand, 'I have no need of you,' nor again the head to the feet, 'I have no need of you.'"

In this passage of Scripture, Paul mentions several things that bear examination. First, he draws attention to the human body, stating how such has many different "members" or functions or moving parts, however you choose to phrase it. The point is, while the body is one, complete organism, it (in and of itself) is not wholly one. For there are many that make up the one. Now again, though there are many members, they are not in disunity, and if they are, it means that the body is sick and dysfunctional. Rather, in a healthy body, though it has many different parts and functions, these all work together in harmony, in unity, as one. When such is accomplished, the body is healthy and operates at peak capacity. Paul begins with this crucial analogy to demonstrate that though there are many moving parts within the Church, they all work together in unison. If one, or many, of the parts (members), are not working together as they ought to, then the Church becomes unhealthy and sick and may eventually die. The first crucial thing, then, to understand is that unity must be the driving force behind all we do for the Church.

Second, Paul states that it is by "one Spirit" that we are all "baptized into one body." This "one Spirit" refers to the Spirit of God, the Holy Spirit, the Spirit of Christ, whichever you prefer. He is drawing attention to the truth that when we received the Holy Spirit, we were engrafted into the one true body, which is the Church. This is what the "baptized into one body" refers to. The word "baptized" is "baptizō" in Greek and it means to immerse, submerge, or overwhelm. Meaning, when we received His Spirit, we were completely immersed in the one body. Not just a portion of

Kingdom Progression

who we are, but all that we are is consumed in the Church.

Third, Paul sought to abolish the notion that any member of the Church was any more significant than another. He stated, "If the foot should say, 'Because I am not a hand, I do not belong to the body,' that would not make it any less a part of the body." Paul here is addressing the sense of pride that so easily sneaks into the Church. We look at those who stand behind the pulpit and glorify them, but it cannot be overstated how grossly wrong this is. You may never be called to stand behind a pulpit, but that doesn't make what you are called to any less significant. The reason this is such a ridiculous idea is pointed out by Paul, "If the whole body were an eye, where would be the sense of hearing? If the whole body were an ear, where would be the sense of smell?" Imagine if all in the Church were called to operate in the same capacity. Imagine if all were called to stand by the pulpit, then who would greet those that come in the door? Who would be the usher? Who would teach the children in Sunday School? Who would play the piano and lead worship? This list of questions could go on forever. The point is if we all did the same thing, the Church would cease to function due to improper balance. Every possible function within the Church must be in proper operation if it is to be the healthy organism God created it to be.

All of this points us back to the vital truth that we need to know our place. We need to know where we fall in the grand scheme of things. We need to know where God has called us so that we can step into that role so that the body can be healthy. There are a few important things we need to understand about this, though. One, discovering your place is only possible through intentional seeking. This requires prayer, reading His Word, and fasting. As well as continued faithfulness in all the areas that we discussed in "Can God Trust You?" Knowing your place is not simply what you would like to do but what you are called to do. What we would like to do is oftentimes what is convenient and easy, but the convenient and easy path is not always the one God calls us to, in fact, it rarely is. He calls us to that which is uncomfortable because it forces us outside of our comfort zone which gives us the space to grow.

Two, we need to understand that, overnight, we are not going to have the full revelation of the call on our lives. God deals in progressive revelation. Meaning, He reveals in due season. Meaning, He is not going to reveal to you your ultimate calling, for you are not ready to bear such a weight. The very thought of walking in that call would likely crush you or cause you to be conceited. Rather, He will reveal a portion of it that draws you closer to the whole. Once you fully operate and dwell in that, He will reveal the next, all along the way, growing your character to become more like Him.

This process can take some time, for we are stubborn creatures that resist that which is painful or causes us to change. Do not rush, for to rush is to step outside the will of God and seek after the "lofty" things on your own accord. This will only lead to your demise. Even if it takes more time than we imagined, we must be patient and allow God to take us down that path of preparation. We talked about this when examining the life of David. God had to take David from a little shepherd boy to a mighty king. This process was painful with many ups and downs, taking somewhere from fourteen to fifteen years. Be patient and allow God to work in you.

Gifts of Service
Romans 12

The first area of spiritual gifts to examine are Gifts of Service, which Paul begins to unveil in Romans chapter twelve.

For by the grace given to me I say to everyone

Kingdom Progression

> among you not to think of himself more highly than he ought to think, but to think with sober judgment, each according to the measure of faith that God has assigned. For as in one body we have many members, and the members do not all have the same function, so we, though many, are one body in Christ, and individually members one of another. Having gifts that differ according to the grace given to us, let us use them: if prophecy, in proportion to our faith; if service, in our serving; the one who teaches, in his teaching; the one who exhorts, in his exhortation; the one who contributes, in generosity; the one who leads, with zeal; the one who does acts of mercy, with cheerfulness.
> -Romans 12:3-8

We talked previously about how we ought to be faithful in service to the Church. If we have a talent in a particular area, we ought to use such for God and His Church. This passage falls into a similar train of thought in the sense that it deals with serving the Church, but these are Gifts of Service that God calls an individual to. Meaning, these areas of service transcend talent.

First, Paul admonishes us to walk in humility. In all that we do we need to ensure that we do not think more highly of ourselves than we ought to. Meaning (going back to the pulpit idea because this is a prevalent misconception), just because you may stand behind a pulpit does not mean you are anything great. You did not earn that spot behind the pulpit; God gave it to you. Just because one stands behind a pulpit does not mean they are greater than another (as we discussed when examining I Corinthians 12:12-21). We need to ensure that no matter where God calls us, we do all things in humility, recognizing that it is God who enabled us to do all that we do anyway. As Paul said, "having gifts that differ according to the grace given to us."

Two, we see that what Paul is addressing here transcends talent or natural ability. We see this to be true based on the wording used by Paul, "according to the grace given to us." "Grace" used here is a word we have looked at previously: "charis." As mentioned previously, it can refer to a few different things, such as, a gift freely given, or the work of God in the life of an individual. What Paul is referring to, then, are Gifts that transcend natural ability and are supernatural. This does not negate what was discussed earlier regarding serving the Church in the areas where our natural ability would allow us. Paul is simply pointing to the truth that God graciously bestows gifts upon us that enable us to serve Him and His Church in an area wherein we would not be able to otherwise.

Paul then proceeds to list some ways in which one could be called to serve. This list is not meant to be exhaustive, rather, more demonstrative. For there are many areas within the body wherein to serve, and those areas of service can and often do overlap. Let's thoroughly examine Paul's list to see what he thought were some prevalent areas in which to serve.

The first area of service mentioned by Paul is "prophecy." This is "prophēteia" in Greek. This word refers to the typically thought definition of prophecy, "prediction of future events (foretelling)." However, this word can refer to more than that, for it can also refer to divinely anointed speaking, speaking under the inspiration of God. What this word could also point to would be ministries involving anointed speaking, which could include a plethora of ministries. Yes, pulpit ministries, but also it could include less thought of ministries like jail ministries or nursing home ministries or such like these. Again, any area of anointed speaking.

"Service" is "diakonia" and it points to several things.

Kingdom Progression

One, it points to one executing the commands of another, or a servant to a master. It also points to the act of serving, as in preparing and serving food. Furthermore, it can also point to the offices that God appoints to proclaim His truth or one who works under those individuals to help them in their roles. Such individuals are often referred to as "deacons." In other words, this act of service points to one who is willing and able to do anything that is asked of them. Whether that is serving food at dinner or working directly alongside one positioned in the Five-Fold Ministry.

"Didaskō" is the word for "teaches," and it means "to hold a discourse with others to instruct them." It can also refer to the office of the Teacher within the Five-Fold Ministry. Either way, the service of teaching (whether that be done by one operating in the Teacher Office or under the teaching anointing) is a much-needed service. One operating in this ministry would be those teaching different classes in the Church, teaching Sunday School, or teaching Home Bible Studies. No matter where the teaching is had, the service of teaching is critical to the Church. The service of teaching requires the teacher to reside in a more personal, one-on-one space with their student. It is in this setting that much learning is accomplished. Much can be learned during service while the preacher is preaching. However, this does not replace the need for personal, one-on-one teaching.

"Exhorts" is "parakaleō," and it means "to console, to encourage and strengthen by consolation, to comfort." There are many areas and ways in which this gift could be acted. There is no shortage of need for encouragement or comfort. Maybe this service refers to one who is always on call for the Pastor of an assembly, ready to encourage and strengthen them. Maybe this refers to one who visits those who are hurting and struggling and can offer them real consolation. There are many ways in which this could be acted, but it is a very real need. For many of the offices and ministries bring with them a heavy weight, and often that heavy weight is too much to bear for the individual. Without one operating in the service of exhortation, it could result in the weight crushing the Pastor or whatever office or ministry needs encouragement. The severity for the need of the operation of this gift cannot be overstated.

Next, we see the service of "contributions." The Greek word here very simply means to give or to impart. What we should thoroughly examine is how one gives. The ESV states that it ought to be done generously. The Greek here is "haplotēs," and it can mean several things that are all crucial to how one is to give. It means liberality, sincerity, generosity, or bountifully. It also means "one who is free from pretense and hypocrisy" and "not self-seeking." Meaning, how this service ought to be acted in is through a sincere desire to help those in need, to freely give, holding nothing back, and to not give with the mind of getting in return or being recognized for their giving. One truly operating in such a gift would likely give anonymously, hoping to avoid being put into the spotlight. Their genuine concern is more toward the individual in need, not themselves.

The word "leads" is "proistēmi," and it refers to all the typical things one thinks of when thinking of leading. This is "residing over, to be set above, to watch over, to protect or guard, to care for," and so on. The one operating as a leader ought to do so with "zeal," which is "spoudē," and it means to earnestly, or diligently do something. Meaning, for the one who leads, they ought not to do so half-heartedly or sluggishly or with no real care for those they lead. Their leading needs to be sincere, done out of genuine care for those under them. The need for those who are called to be leaders is very real. Some may think that we don't need leaders and that we can simply figure everything out collectively. This will only lead to chaos. For there will be so many different voices and opinions and no one to mediate between all those differing ideas. There must be those who are called by God to stand up and give proper direction: those who can hear all

Kingdom Progression

the ideas and thoughts and by the grace of God determine the best path forward.

Lastly, then, is the service of "mercy." "Eleeō" is the Greek here, and it simply refers to mercy or compassion. This is also a very real need within the Church. For, as stated previously, many may be struggling and hurting, and they need more than just encouragement: they need someone to show them true compassion. Webster's Dictionary defines compassion as "a suffering with another; painful sympathy; a sensation of sorrow excited by the distress or misfortunes of another; pity; commiseration. Compassion is a mixed passion, compounded of love and sorrow." Meaning, one operating in this gift is sensitive to what others are experiencing, whether that be sorrow or joy, and experiences such with them. They weep with those who weep and shout with those who rejoice. To sit by and watch those who suffer, and to let them do so alone, will only lead to their destruction. They need those who will come alongside them and say, "You're not alone."

All of the gifts of service mentioned here by Paul ought to be operated in some degree by every mature man and woman of God. These are all acts of grace we ought to dwell in. However, some are more gifted in some of these areas than others. Some are more gifted to lead due to the grace of God expounding in that area: same for the gift of teaching. Some are called in greater measure to teach. This does not excuse those of us who may not have the same level of grace at work in us in that area. The NIV translates the last line of verse 3 as, "in accordance with the faith God has distributed to each of you." The original Greek confirms this train of thought. God has given all the ability according to their faith to operate in all these gifts. Meaning, as our faith grows, so should our ability to operate in the different gifts of service. The greater the faith, the greater one serves others.

Kristopher David Grepke

I Peter 4

Keeping in line with the gifts of service, Peter also gave additional teaching regarding such. He wrote this in his first epistle:

> The end of all things is at hand; therefore be self-controlled and sober-minded for the sake of your prayers. Above all, keep loving one another earnestly, since love covers a multitude of sins. Show hospitality to one another without grumbling. As each has received a gift, use it to serve one another, as good stewards of God's varied grace: whoever speaks, as one who speaks oracles of God; whoever serves, as one who serves by the strength that God supplies—in order that in everything God may be glorified through Jesus Christ. To him belong glory and dominion forever and ever. Amen.
> -I Peter 4:7-11

First, the Apostle Peter admonishes us to be "self-controlled" and "sober-minded." "Self-controlled" is "sōphroneō," and it is quite ironic, for this word more accurately means "sober-minded" than the word used for "sober-minded." This word means "to be of a sound mind," or "to be in one's right mind." It can also refer to having the mindset and attitude of humility, not thinking more highly of yourself than you ought to. This word for "sober-minded" is "nēphō," and it means, "to be sober," or "free from intoxication." As pointed out when discussing one's character, the idea of being sober or free from intoxication goes beyond just being free from alcohol. It refers more so to simply being free from any life-dominating influence, be it drugs, alcohol, pornography, or so on. What we see here from

Kingdom Progression

Peter is, as starters, the need to be diligent and intentional in ensuring that we remain humble and in a controlled state of mind in all that we do. In addition to that, we need to ensure that we are free from all outward influences that would gain control over us and dominate us. For if we are being controlled or dominated by an outside force other than God, He cannot use us in the capacity which He desires. The need for this soundness of mind and sobriety grows even more as "the end of all things" approaches. It is also interesting, for Peter specifically states that we need to actively ensure that we are in step with these things "for the sake of your prayers." Implying, then, that if we do not remain humble with a sound mind and abstain from all life-dominating influences, our prayers will be hindered. Or in other words, God will not hear us or communicate with us.

Peter then goes on to state that earnest love and sincere hospitality must also be present. However, not just to be present, for he states, "above all." Meaning, love and hospitality must be what drive us. First, Peter states that "love covers a multitude of sins." This is not to say that gross sins are swept under the rug, so to speak, for the sake of love. For that is not love. Love corrects the sinner to draw them unto repentance. What Peter is saying here is that where love is absent, judgment will abound. Meaning, there will be disunity and discord and fighting and the Church will be torn apart. On the other hand, where there is love, there is mercy. Love says, "I know you didn't mean to: I forgive you." This is what Peter was pointing to: love does not hold a grudge, rather, love forgives. Second, he stated the need for "hospitality…without grumbling." "Hospitality" is "philoxenos," and it refers to one who is "kind to strangers," or "fond of guests." Meaning, it is one who is welcoming. It is easy to put on a face of "welcoming" but on the inside be full of discontentment and strife and anger. It is easy to say, "I'm so happy to see you!" While truly meaning, "Why are you here?" True hospitality seeks to welcome those around them. True hospitality is inviting.

We must examine these qualities mentioned by the Apostle Peter, for he gave these qualities before speaking on different gifts of service one may operate in. Meaning, Peter was stating that for one to operate in the grace of God, one must first abide in these mentalities and attitudes, that is, humility and soundness of mind, sobriety, genuine love that forgives, and welcoming hospitality.

Peter mentions only two specific gifts of service, but one could argue that these two gifts mentioned vaguely cover all services. First, he points to those who speak, but they do not speak of their own accord, rather, they speak the "oracles of God." "Oracles" is "logion," and it refers to a divine communication or revelation. Meaning, those who speak, do not speak unless they expressly hear from God. For if you stand up to speak but have not heard from God, you will only be speaking out of yourself. Such a one speaking only of themselves and not of God would contradict the very purpose for the gift of speaking, "in order that in everything God may be glorified." Two, he then draws attention to those that serve. Similar to how he stated that those who speak ought to speak through revelation from God, he also states that those who serve ought to serve by the strength of God. Meaning, our serving ought to be empowered by God. Meaning, what Peter is stating here is doing things that are outside our realm of comfortability, because when we do them, all people will know that we did not do them according to ourselves or our ability, but they will know that it was God working in us. Again, "in order that in everything God may be glorified."

The Apostle Peter also stated the "why" behind every act of service: "to serve one another." "Serve" here is "diakoneō," and it relates to a variety of things, all pointing to doing something for another for their sake, to help them. Meaning, all that we do, we do for those around us: our brothers and sisters in Christ and for those who are not yet

Kingdom Progression

here with us. We must remember that all that we do is for others. This must be the mentality we keep at all times, in all things. Every gift you operate in, every office you serve in, and every title you hold, is all for the sake of those around you.

Gifts of the Spirit

Now that we have examined I Corinthians 12:12-21 (knowing your place in the Church), Romans 12:3-8 (operating in the gifts of service within the Church), and I Peter 4:7-11 (dwelling in the proper mindset and attitude and acting out of the proper motivations to rightly serve others) can we truly begin to examine the Gifts of the Spirit and then the Five-Fold Ministry in the following chapter.

Paul began his discourse on the Gifts of the Spirit by stating, "Now concerning spiritual gifts, brothers, I do not want you to be uninformed" (I Corinthians 11:1). He goes on to explain how the Corinthian Church largely came from a background of paganism, worshipping false idols and such. Meaning, due to their background and previous experience, the Apostle Paul was afraid that they may misuse and abuse the Gifts of the Spirit. To avoid such, he wrote to them the following:

> Now there are varieties of gifts, but the same Spirit; and there are varieties of service, but the same Lord; and there are varieties of activities, but it is the same God who empowers them all in everyone. To each is given the manifestation of the Spirit for the common good. For to one is given through the Spirit the utterance of wisdom, and to another the utterance of knowledge according to the same Spirit, to another faith by the same Spirit, to another gifts of healing by the one

> Spirit, to another the working of miracles, to another prophecy, to another the ability to distinguish between spirits, to another various kinds of tongues, to another the interpretation of tongues. All these are empowered by one and the same Spirit, who apportions to each one individually as he wills.
> -I Corinthians 11:4-11

Paul begins by emphatically conveying that the Gifts of the Spirit are expressly empowered by God and God alone. Thus, he began his lesson by tearing down the false idea that these gifts were only given to those who were "special," or that certain individuals were born with such gifts. Rather, he conveyed that it is God and God alone who grants these gifts. In this, he also implied that it is only those who abide in His Spirit that can operate in these gifts. For he states that it is the "same Spirit." If the Spirit does not abide in an individual, they cannot operate in the gifts, meaning, if they are claiming to operate in such but have not received His Spirit, it is false. For, "no one can say, 'Jesus is Lord' except by the Holy Spirit" (I Corinthians 11:3).

We also see that "to each is given," which means all who have been born of the Spirit can be used in each of these gifts. Some have the misconception that certain of these gifts are only for certain individuals, but this is not the case. There are gifts that we more naturally operate in, due to how they correlate to our personality, but this does not mean we are unable to operate in them all. We are admonished by Paul, at the close of I Corinthians 12, to "earnestly desire the higher gifts" (v.31). "Higher" is a poor translation of this word. It is "kreittōn," and it more accurately refers to what is more useful, profitable, or advantageous. Meaning, different gifts are needed based on what is currently happening. Paul here is admonishing us that when we see a present need to earnestly seek after the Gift of the Spirit that would best

Kingdom Progression

meet that need. This then informs us as to the purpose of the Gifts of the Spirit: they are given at specific points in time to meet specific needs. It is not that an individual walks in a particular gift every moment of their life, but that at precise moments God will grant the precise gift to meet the precise need. This is why Paul admonished us to seek after that which is most advantageous because every situation will be met with a gift. Contained within this Scripture is the truth that we are capable of operating in every gift (if we have been Born Again), or else he would not have admonished all to seek after that which is needed.

We also see here another reason for these gifts, that is, they are for the "common good" (v.7). Once again pointing to the truth that every gift is not for our personal benefit, it is for and about those around us. Now, this does include us, for we are a part of the Body. However, it is not expressly about us. We need to ensure that we maintain the heart of a servant in all that we do for His Kingdom.

Here is the list of the nine Gifts of the Spirit that we see (I will be naming them according to the KJV, as that is the most recognizable terminology attributed to these Gifts.):

- Word of Wisdom
- Word of Knowledge
- Gift of Faith
- Gifts of Healing
- Working of Miracles
- Gift of Prophecy
- Discerning of Spirits
- Divers Kinds of Tongues
- Interpretation of Tongues

We are going to break these down so that we may understand them in a greater way, because the better we understand them, the better we will be able to properly operate in them and avoid misuse and abuse. Again, quoting the Apostle Paul, "I do not want you to be uninformed." The nine Gifts of the Spirit are often condensed into three categories, that is:

Gifts of Revelation:
  -Word of Wisdom
  -Word of Knowledge
  -Discerning of Spirits

Gifts of Power:
  -Gift of Faith
  -Working of Miracles
  -Gifts of Healing

Gifts of Utterance (Speaking):
  -Gift of Prophecy
  -Divers Kinds of Tongues
  -Interpretation of Tongues

In our examination of the Gifts of the Spirit, we are simply going to look at them as Paul ordered them.

Word of Wisdom

The first gift mentioned by the Apostle Paul is the Gift of Wisdom. "Wisdom" here is "sophia." "Sophia" is a very broad word, covering a wide range of definitions surrounding wisdom. Some examples are: practical wisdom; superior knowledge and enlightenment; divine wisdom; and revealed wisdom. This word can also refer to the gift of interpreting dreams and visions. Webster's Dictionary defines "wisdom" as, "the right use or exercise of knowledge." This is oftentimes how I have heard it defined by my Pastor: "Wisdom is knowledge applied."

Taking all of this into consideration, some proper and simple definitions of wisdom that we could surmise would be guidance, or direction. What we then understand about

Kingdom Progression

the Gift of Wisdom, then, is that it is God directly leading an individual. This is divine wisdom though, so this also implies that how God directs and guides the individual is far beyond their ability. We also see, though, that "sophia" can refer to the interpretation of dreams or visions. Therefore, God's Gift of Wisdom could also be Him divinely revealing the true purpose or meaning of a dream or vision. Dreams or visions are often given to us to provide direction or guidance, so this plays into our simplified definition of wisdom.

We see that specifically this gift is a Word of Wisdom. "Word" is "logos" which refers to a word, or an utterance. Meaning, when God grants this gift to an individual, it is not an eternal outpouring of all of His divine wisdom. Rather, it is a word for that specific moment. Meaning, God grants wisdom when there is a need for such, but operating in this gift does not give access to the individual to understand all the wisdom of God. This wisdom is but a portion.

Looking at the Book of Acts, we see several examples of this Gift in operation. We will examine two of them here.

> And they went through the region of Phrygia and Galatia, having been forbidden by the Holy Spirit to speak the word in Asia. And when they had come up to Mysia, they attempted to go into Bithynia, but the Spirit of Jesus did not allow them. So, passing by Mysia, they went down to Troas. And a vision appeared to Paul in the night: a man of Macedonia was standing there, urging him and saying, "Come over to Macedonia and help us." And when Paul had seen the vision, immediately we sought to go on into Macedonia, concluding that God had called us to preach the gospel to them.
> -Acts 16:6-10

Kristopher David Grepke

Here is what we see from this passage. Paul is on his second missionary journey with Silas and Timothy accompanying him. Paul had in his mind a specific path that he wanted to follow in his journey. His motives were not ill or poor motives, for he simply wanted to preach the Gospel. However, there was something that he did not know or see because it was beyond his ability to know and see such. The Bible then says, "The Spirit of Jesus did not allow them." How exactly this looked, we do not know. It states that they tried to go into Bithynia, but there was just something that would not allow them. Due to this, they altered their course, and that night a vision was given to Paul that provided divine direction. In this passage we see the Gift of Wisdom working in two different ways: one, it hindered them from proceeding down the wrong path, and two, it gave proper direction to the correct path. We see, then, that a Word of Wisdom can both stop an individual from a present course of action and guide them to the proper course.

> Since they had been without food for a long time, Paul stood up among them and said, "Men, you should have listened to me and not have set sail from Crete and incurred this injury and loss. Yet now I urge you to take heart, for there will be no loss of life among you, but only of the ship. For this very night there stood before me an angel of the God to whom I belong and whom I worship, and he said, 'Do not be afraid, Paul; you must stand before Caesar. And behold, God has granted you all those who sail with you.' So take heart, men, for I have faith in God that it will be exactly as I have been told. But we must run aground on some island.
> -Acts 27:21-26

Kingdom Progression

Here in chapter twenty-seven of the Book of Acts, we read of a shipwreck that Paul experienced. Throughout this particular event, several gifts were at work in the life of Paul, but here specifically we once again see the Gift of Wisdom at work. For the men of the ship found themselves amid a great storm and fearing for their lives. However, in the middle of the night, God appeared to Paul and granted him a Word of Wisdom, informing him of the events to come and that all would survive if they obeyed the wisdom of God. There was no way Paul could have directed these men unless he had first been directed.

Later in the same story, we read of several men attempting to escape, thinking they had a better chance on their own than with the ship. Paul saw them and declared, "Unless these men stay in the ship, you cannot be saved" (Acts 27:31). Again, we see God give a Word of Wisdom to and through Paul, for he had no way of knowing that staying on the ship would save their lives other than the divine guidance of God.

Word of Knowledge

The second gift mentioned by Paul is the Word of Knowledge. The Word of Knowledge and the Word of Wisdom often go hand-in-hand. One could use the expression that they are "two sides of the same coin." Where there is one, there is often the other, but this is not always the case. However, we see this oftentimes being the case due to what I said about wisdom: wisdom is knowledge applied.

"Knowledge" here is "gnōsis," and it is the basic definition of knowledge, referring to "general understanding or intelligence, or advanced learning." Webster's Dictionary defines "knowledge" as "a clear and certain perception of the truth and facts." In regards to this specific Gift of the Spirit, we understand a Word of Knowledge to be understanding that is revealed to an individual regarding something that they did not know. Others may know this particular truth or fact, but the individual to whom it is revealed has no prior understanding of such.

Again, we see that this is a "word" which is the same word from the Word of Wisdom. Meaning, this is once again just a portion of God's understanding. It is a precise understanding of a particular subject given at a precise moment and time to meet a precise need. If God were to reveal all His understanding, it would be too great for us to bear, for we are told at several points throughout Scripture that He sees and knows all (see Psalms 147:5; I John 3:20).

We will again examine two portions of Scripture that highlight this gift in action, both once again from the Book of Acts.

> But a man named Ananias, with his wife Sapphira, sold a piece of property, and with his wife's knowledge he kept back for himself some of the proceeds and brought only a part of it and laid it at the apostles' feet. But Peter said, "Ananias, why has Satan filled your heart to lie to the Holy Spirit and to keep back for yourself part of the proceeds of the land? While it remained unsold, did it not remain your own? And after it was sold, was it not at your disposal? Why is it that you have contrived this deed in your heart? You have not lied to man but to God." When Ananias heard these words, he fell down and breathed his last. And great fear came upon all who heard of it. The young men rose and wrapped him up and carried him out and buried him. After an interval of about three hours his wife came in, not knowing what had happened. And Peter said to her, "Tell me whether you sold the land for so much." And

> she said, "Yes, for so much." But Peter said to her, "How is it that you have agreed together to test the Spirit of the Lord? Behold, the feet of those who have buried your husband are at the door, and they will carry you out." Immediately she fell down at his feet and breathed her last. When the young men came in they found her dead, and they carried her out and buried her beside her husband.
> -Acts 5:1-10

The context of this passage comes from chapter four of the Book of Acts which tells us of how the Church was coming together in unprecedented ways to provide for those in need among the Church. Many were selling all their land and giving all the proceeds to the Apostles to distribute as needed. Then we see Ananias and Sapphira conspire in their hearts to do the same but lie about the amount. They did this in secret, so there was no possible way the Apostle Peter could have known of this attempted deception except by the Word of Knowledge. God revealed to Peter what they had done in secret and when he confronted them about such, they agreed to lie. Thus, sealing their judgement.

> Since much time had passed, and the voyage was now dangerous because even the Fast was already over, Paul advised them, saying, "Sirs, I perceive that the voyage will be with injury and much loss, not only of the cargo and the ship, but also of our lives." But the centurion paid more attention to the pilot and to the owner of the ship than to what Paul said. And because the harbor was not suitable to spend the winter in, the majority decided to put out to sea from there, on the chance that somehow they could reach Phoenix, a

harbor of Crete, facing both southwest and northwest, and spend the winter there.
-Acts 27:9-12

The second example takes us back to the story of the shipwreck from chapter twenty-seven. As we follow the Book of Acts and read about the lives of the individuals whom we follow, never once do we read that Paul was educated in the area of sailing. We do read that he was a tent maker by trade, so I imagine he knew much about this. However, he was not an educated sailor, especially when compared to the combined experience of those leading the ship (the pilot and owner of the ship). It was in this situation that God then gave Paul a Word of Knowledge, informing him of the danger to come due to the inclement weather at hand. Paul had no way of knowing such things except by divine understanding.

Gift of Faith

Hearing that there is a Gift of Faith may seem confusing at first, for we have discussed the importance of faith previously, and in such we discussed how if we have no faith we cannot please God (see Hebrews 11:6), for faith is what enables us to expect what is not seen (see Hebrews 11:1). Paul also tells us, "for in it the righteousness of God is revealed from faith for faith, as it is written, 'The righteous shall live by faith'" (Romans 1:17). We have also seen, when examining the New Birth, how faith must be present or else it is in vain. Faith must accompany repentance, believing that He is faithful and just to forgive us (see I John 1:9). And faith must also accompany water baptism, believing that His sacrifice truly covered all our sins, both past, present, and future (see Acts 8:36-38). Additionally, faith must accompany receiving His Spirit, for such is a very supernatural act that requires great faith in His resurrection (see Galatians 3:2).

Why then does Paul say that faith is a Gift of the

Kingdom Progression

Spirit? One must understand that there is a difference between the faith that a Born Again child of God walks in every day, and the faith mentioned here. We will define the faith that we all walk in every day as fundamental faith. "Fundamental" means, "serving for the foundation," according to Webster's Dictionary. We will, then, define the Gift of Faith as, exponential faith. "Exponential" means "(of an increase) becoming more and more rapid," according to Oxford Languages.

The Gift of Faith is an increased level of faith beyond the foundational level to bring an individual through a situation. This can look different based on the situation. Meaning, the Gift of Faith could increase the faith of the individual so that a great miracle might be performed in their midst that would not have been performed if not for the increased level of faith. Or it could mean an increased level of faith to increase the individual's level of trust in God (for trust often goes hand-in-hand with faith: if faith increases, trust increases) amid a situation that is difficult beyond the individual's ability to bear.

We will examine two examples from the Book of Acts that demonstrate these two different thoughts.

In Acts 6:5 we are first introduced to a man named Stephen. He is described as being a man "full of faith." "Full" is "plērēs" which means, "full of, abounding in, wholly occupied with, completely under the influence of, or affected by." Meaning, Stephen did not dwell simply at the fundamental level of faith; rather, he regularly operated in a place of exponential faith. Knowing such about Stephen, we then read this passage:

> Now when they heard these things they were enraged, and they ground their teeth at him. But he, full of the Holy Spirit, gazed into heaven and saw the glory of God, and Jesus standing at the right hand of God. And he

> said, "Behold, I see the heavens opened, and the Son of Man standing at the right hand of God." But they cried out with a loud voice and stopped their ears and rushed together at him. Then they cast him out of the city and stoned him. And the witnesses laid down their garments at the feet of a young man named Saul. And as they were stoning Stephen, he called out, "Lord Jesus, receive my spirit." And falling to his knees he cried out with a loud voice, "Lord, do not hold this sin against them." And when he had said this, he fell asleep.
> -Acts 7:54-60

Here we see demonstrated the second manner in which the Gift of Faith could work in an individual's life that I mentioned earlier: to increase their trust in God amid a difficult situation. Many in Stephen's shoes would have succumbed to fear and horror. Fearing the thought of losing their life and fearing the painful death that he endured. Interestingly, we see no such fear in Stephen. Rather, we see him looking to heaven, surrounded by gritting teeth and enraged glances. And even while being dragged out of the city and stoned, he did not cry out for mercy from the men but cried out for reception from Jesus. To top all of this off, he prayed for his persecutors while they yet stoned him.

> On the first day of the week, when we were gathered together to break bread, Paul talked with them, intending to depart on the next day, and he prolonged his speech until midnight. There were many lamps in the upper room where we were gathered. And a young man named Eutychus, sitting at the window, sank into a deep sleep as Paul talked

Kingdom Progression

still longer. And being overcome by sleep, he fell down from the third story and was taken up dead. But Paul went down and bent over him, and taking him in his arms, said, "Do not be alarmed, for his life is in him." And when Paul had gone up and had broken bread and eaten, he conversed with them a long while, until daybreak, and so departed. And they took the youth away alive, and were not a little comforted.
-Acts 20:7-12

Here in this second example, we see the Gift of Faith lead to the miraculous. For we read of how Eutychus fell from a third-story window and was taken up dead. Luke was present for this event (evident by the pronoun "we"), so it is likely he was the one to pronounce him dead, due to him being a physician. This pronunciation of death did not stop Paul from ceasing his discourse to the people and running to the young boy. We are told that he "bent over him" and took "him in his arms." It is not expressly stated that Paul prayed over the lifeless young man, but it is easy to surmise such when examining the ministry of Paul across the Book of Acts. What is interesting is that it does not state that Eutychus immediately sprang to life, yet Paul still spoke in faith, "Do not be alarmed, for his life is in him." Although it was not seen, he believed. Exponential faith! Later we read that the young man awoke and they "took the youth away alive." Not every miracle of God is going to be instantaneous, but in the times that it is not, it is the Gift of Faith that carries us through to fruition.

Gifts of Healing

This Gift of the Spirit is immediately interesting due to how it stands apart from the other gifts, for this is one of the only gifts expressed in the plural form, Gifts of Healing. We will examine this momentarily, first, we need to understand what healing means. "Healing" here is "iama" which can mean either healing or cure. There are several different ways one could define cure, for it could refer to an antidote for a disease or poison or the general restoration of health from a disease or wound. The Webster's Dictionary gives a definition of such that I particularly enjoy, that is, "to subdue, remove, destroy or put an end to."

This is how we will be defining healing: subduing, removing, destroying, or putting an end to it. What exactly do the Gifts of Healing do such to? This is where the plural, gifts, comes into play. For by Paul stating that there were Gifts of Healing he was implying that there was more than one area that can be healed. For example, there can be emotional healing, mental healing, spiritual healing, and physical healing. One could also say that he stated there were Gifts of Healing because divine healing does not have to look the same way every time.

There are many examples throughout Scripture of various kinds of healings being performed in different ways. Staying in the New Testament, we can examine the Gospels and the Book of Acts to see a plethora of examples of such. For example, we see Jesus heal different blind men in various ways. We see one instance wherein He simply touched the eyes of the blind man (see Matthew 9:27-20). We also see Him spitting in the eyes of the blind and then touching them (see Mark 8:22-25). Another wherein He simply spoke to the individual (see Mark 10:46-52). Finally, we see Him spit in the mud and then rub the mud in the eyes of the blind (see John 9:6).

However, I specifically want to look at an example that demonstrates how the Gifts of Healing reaches beyond just the physical and into the other areas mentioned (emotional, mental, and spiritual). When we hear "healing" our minds automatically gravitate toward the physical, for this is the

Kingdom Progression

most evident form of healing. This is dangerous because it causes us to become stuck in a box, further, it causes us to force God into a box. We need to understand that the Gifts of Healing are given to subdue, remove, destroy, and put an end to all afflictions.

> The scribes and the Pharisees brought a woman who had been caught in adultery and placing her in the midst they said to him, "Teacher, this woman has been caught in the act of adultery. Now in the Law, Moses commanded us to stone such women. So what do you say?" This they said to test him, that they might have some charge to bring against him. Jesus bent down and wrote with his finger on the ground. And as they continued to ask him, he stood up and said to them, "Let him who is without sin among you be the first to throw a stone at her." And once more he bent down and wrote on the ground. But when they heard it, they went away one by one, beginning with the older ones, and Jesus was left alone with the woman standing before him. Jesus stood up and said to her, "Woman, where are they? Has no one condemned you?" She said, "No one, Lord." And Jesus said, "Neither do I condemn you; go, and from now on sin no more.
> -John 8:3-11

This is a story we all know well, the adulterer that He saved from judgment. We read this story and rejoice over His mercy and love, which we ought to. However, there is an integral aspect of this story that we glance over because it is not readily right in front of us. Imagine with me the state of this woman on the levels mentioned previously: emotionally, mentally, and spiritually. She was actively caught in adultery, meaning, something was going on inwardly that was driving this woman toward self-destruction. On top of that, you are dragged into a crowd of judging eyes and mouths, with the threat of death hanging over your head. Most of us probably cannot even begin to imagine the state this woman was in.

We read of how Jesus expertly thwarted her accusers by drawing attention to their sins, demonstrating how they are not worthy to determine who deserves life or death. After the crowd dissipates, Jesus bends down and begins to speak to the woman, "Where are they?" Those that were driving her toward destruction had been removed, the accusations had been put to an end, and her judgment subdued. She recognized the removal of such, and then He makes a tantalizing statement, "Neither do I condemn you; go, and from now on sin no more." Her past that had bound her and condemned her to die was no more. She was free from her accusers and her past. In other words, she had been divinely healed.

There is one additional thing that ought to be discussed when speaking on the Gifts of the Healing. When we seek after the demonstration of this gift, we cannot forsake our faith and trust in God. There will be times when we pray for the sick or the afflicted to be healed and delivered, and they aren't. Such instances cause many to fall out of their faith in God, but this is because their faith was already practically non-existent. As discussed when speaking on faith, there are times when situations don't go the way that seems the "most beneficial." Like with Stephen: Why did God not step in and deliver him? Why did He let him die? In these moments we must remember that God has a divine will and plan for every situation. If He does not heal an individual, we cannot lose faith and trust in Him. Rather, we need to recognize that He has a plan behind not healing them. Perhaps it is time for them to come home (home in the sense of eternally in His presence). Or maybe a tragic event is what will draw another

Kingdom Progression

unto God in repentance. There are things we don't see. This is not to say that we should not seek the Gifts of Healing. We ought to always seek such. At the same time, we must also recognize that He is in control, and He knows what He is doing.

Working of Miracles

We see here another Gift of the Spirit expressed in the plural form. The plurality that this Gift dwells in is different than the Gifts of the Healing though. The plurality attributed to the Gifts of Healing expresses that there are multiple gifts within this one gift (we examined how the Gifts of Healing encompassed emotional, mental, spiritual, and physical healing); the plurality attributed to the Working of Miracles, though, implies abundance. Meaning, miracles should not be viewed as a distant thing of the past or a rare occurrence. Rather, miracles should be expected and expected abundantly.

Webster's Dictionary defines a miracle as, "an event or effects contrary to the established constitution and course of things, or a deviation from the known laws of nature; a supernatural event." Typically, we would define healing as part of the miracle category. However, by Paul separating the Working of Miracles from the Gifts of Healing, it is understood that this specifically refers to something apart from divine healing. This is affirmed when one examines the Greek behind the word "miracles." This word is "dunamis," and it more rightly means "power," and different adjectives attributed to power. The word "working" is "energēma" which means "working" or "operation." This Gift of the Spirit, then, is best understood as the working (or operation) of divine power. Meaning, it is God working through the individual to accomplish feats far beyond their physical ability.

There are several examples throughout the Book of

Acts of this gift in action. One such example is found after Philip baptized the Ethiopian Eunuch.

> And when they came up out of the water, the Spirit of the Lord carried Philip away, and the eunuch saw him no more, and went on his way rejoicing. But Philip found himself at Azotus, and as he passed through he preached the gospel to all the towns until he came to Caesarea.
> -Acts 8:39-40

What we see transpire in this passage seems to be a sort of divine teleportation. How this looked exactly, we don't know. Whether it was Philip disappearing in one place and then appearing in another, or if it was a rapid transition, we don't know. What we do know is the language used in this passage implies it was something that transcended the natural order. For His Spirit carried Philip away in such a manner that the eunuch simply didn't see him any longer, implying that he disappeared from before his eyes. Then Philip "found himself," meaning, the transition was so rapid that he had to take a moment to get his bearings and figure out where he was.

Another powerful example of this gift in operation is the well-known story of Paul and Silas in prison.

> About midnight Paul and Silas were praying and singing hymns to God, and the prisoners were listening to them, and suddenly there was a great earthquake, so that the foundations of the prison were shaken. And immediately all the doors were opened, and everyone's bonds were unfastened. When the jailer woke and saw that the prison doors were open, he drew his sword and was about to kill himself,

Kingdom Progression

> supposing that the prisoners had escaped. But Paul cried with a loud voice, "Do not harm yourself, for we are all here." And the jailer called for lights and rushed in, and trembling with fear he fell down before Paul and Silas. Then he brought them out and said, "Sirs, what must I do to be saved?"
> -Acts 16:25-30

Amid bondage and imprisonment, Paul and Silas, instead of being overcome with doubt and fear and worry, began to lift prayer and praise unto God. What they prayed, and what they sang, we do not know. What we do know is that faith was at the center of such, because God was in the midst of it. While they yet prayed and sang, an earthquake immediately manifested, shaking the entire foundation of the prison. Notice that it did not destroy the prison or threaten the lives of the prisoners, it did just enough. For it shook the doors open and somehow broke the chains holding the prisoners captive. This was no ordinary earthquake. This was the power of God on full display, as we defined the Working of Miracles. Also, notice what happened because of this display of power: it brought about salvation.

In our day and age, miracles have become the abnormal, the oddity. People talk about miracles and those around them look at them with speculation. We speak of miracles and others immediately tune us out due to thinking that we are crazy. We have become so consumed in the natural order that we forget that we serve a God that transcends the natural order, for He created such. The idea of healing isn't so crazy in our culture, but the idea that one could be transported from one location to another? Or that one could walk on water? These are fairy tales to us, but they shouldn't be. I'm not saying that God will just magically transport you for no reason or allow you to walk on water just because. When God displays His power through us there is a distinct purpose as to why. Meaning, when a need is present that requires His power, and our faith is present to allow it, He will perform the miraculous through us.

Jesus Himself said, "And these signs will accompany those who believe: in my name they will cast out demons; they will speak in new tongues; they will pick up serpents with their hands; and if they drink any deadly poison, it will not hurt them; they will lay their hands on the sick, and they will recover" (Mark 16:17-18). The Working of Miracles ought to follow the one who claims to walk in faith in Him. This is not to say that we can idly sit by and do nothing while we watch miracles transpire in our lives. Paul stated that one who does not work should not receive even the necessities of life (see II Thessalonians 3:10). Also, James specifically stated that true faith is always accompanied by genuine works (see James 2:14-26). The Working of Miracles cannot be our excuse to not work, but we should also walk in genuine faith, understanding that God can and will do the miraculous to accomplish His Will if the need is present. There must be balance. For God will not give the miraculous if we are not readily working.

Gift of Prophecy

The Gift of Prophecy carries some confusion with it, which we aim to address before we dive into what this gift looks like in operation. The confusion that surrounds this gift is what exactly it refers to. For if you examine the Greek word, "prophēteia," it can refer to a couple of different things. On one end, this word can refer to any sort of divine utterance. In this case, prophecy could refer to any degree of anointed speaking: preaching, teaching, or prophesying. We looked at this when we examined the passage from Romans 12, one of the services that some are gifted in is prophecy. We broke this down to mean anointed speaking. This is not what Paul is referring to here, for the Gifts of the Spirit

Kingdom Progression

refer to gifts from God that are specifically for very precise moments to meet specific needs, as discussed previously. If this gift, then, referred to any degree of anointed speaking, it would not fall under the Gifts of the Spirit. This then tells us that Paul was aiming to be much more specific when he mentioned the Gift of Prophecy. Understanding this, we look to the other meanings of the Greek word, "revealing hidden things."

Prophecy is very intricate, for people usually only think of it as foretelling, which is a prediction of future events. We do see this displayed throughout Scripture. However, another aspect of prophecy that is often not understood or realized is its forth-telling aspect. While foretelling, as stated, predicts (or reveals) future things to come, forth-telling reveals past or present things. Understanding such, we will define the Gift of Prophecy as revealing through divine revelation.

It is also important to understand that this gift is different than the office of the prophet. We will in-depth explore what the office of the prophet looks like in the next chapter, so I will not do so here. As stated, the Gifts of the Spirit work to meet specific needs. Meaning, just because one prophecies on an occasion does not mean they are a prophet. It simply means they allowed God to use them at that moment in time for the specific need.

In addition, when God uses an individual in the Gift of Prophecy, rarely does He fully reveal every aspect of the situation to the individual. Meaning, God uses them to speak the divinely inspired word but may not fully reveal to them its meaning. This is particularly true when a prophecy is given to a specific individual rather than on a corporate (Church Body) level. One example from the Book of Acts stands out in this regard.

> When we had come in sight of Cyprus, leaving it on the left we sailed to Syria and landed

> at Tyre, for there the ship was to unload its cargo. And having sought out the disciples, we stayed there for seven days. And through the Spirit they were telling Paul not to go on to Jerusalem.
> -Acts 21:3-4

Many read this passage and think it to mean that God was telling Paul to not go to Jerusalem through the Gift of Prophecy. But if we examine the context of this passage among the others wherein Paul's journey to Jerusalem was mentioned, we see that Paul was utterly convinced that God had already called him to go to Jerusalem (see Acts 21:13). Those around him thought this meant that he was not to go. However, Paul understood it personally as a warning that danger awaited him, for he stated that he was ready to die for Him. Therefore, while no one else truly understood the word of God, Paul did, for it was for him specifically.

In this same chapter of the Book of Acts, we also see mentioned four daughters of the Evangelist (the way it is attributed to him it seems as though he operated in the Office of the Evangelist) Philip. Specifically, we read that these four daughters were known to prophesy. Notice the wording though: it did not label them as prophets (as in the Five-Fold Ministry) but simply that they prophesied. It is as I said, there are certain gifts that we are more prone to, so it appears that these daughters were prone to this specific gift.

Also contained within this same chapter is one who operated in the Office of the Prophet, Agabus, who confirmed that bondage awaited Paul in Jerusalem (he confirms what Paul understood in that he was to go to Jerusalem but imprisonment awaited him [see Acts 21:10-12]).

Discerning of Spirits

The gift of Discerning of Spirits is another widely

misunderstood Gift of the Spirit. Many misinterpret this gift as simple discernment. Discernment is defined by Webster's Dictionary as "the power or faculty of the mind, by which it distinguishes one thing from another, as truth from falsehood, virtue from vice; acuteness of judgment; the power of perceiving differences of things or ideas, and their relations and tendencies." Meaning, anyone can discern, for another way to define discernment is simply perception. That is often how individuals think of this gift: that it is simply a heightened perception. This is not the case.

The part that many overlook regarding this gift is that it specifically refers to the spiritual world, hence the Discerning of Spirits. What are different aspects of the spiritual that an individual could discern? There are three basic realms (if that is the correct terminology) of the spiritual: God and His angels, Satan and his demons, and the human spirit (or in other words, the personal will of the individual). What we come to understand, then, is that the Discerning of Spirits is divine insight or revelation as to which aspect of the spiritual realm is motivating a current course of action. Is God driving this path forward according to His Will? Is Satan attempting to lead one astray into destruction? Or is it the human will at work, simply doing what they want to?

There is a deeper level to the Discerning of Spirits though, and that is an insight into which spirit exactly is at work. Meaning, is it the Spirit of Love, Peace, Unity, or Holiness (which are all of one Spirit, which is the Spirit of God, but different aspects of that One Spirit)? Or is it the spirit of lust, greed, or strife at work? These are just a few examples of course, there are many specific spirits that could be at work.

There are several prominent examples of this Gift we see from the Book of Acts.

> He was with the proconsul, Sergius Paulus, a
> man of intelligence, who summoned Barnabas

> and Saul and sought to hear the word of God. But Elymas the magician (for that is the meaning of his name) opposed them, seeking to turn the proconsul away from the faith. But Saul, who was also called Paul, filled with the Holy Spirit, looked intently at him and said, "You son of the devil, you enemy of all righteousness, full of all deceit and villainy, will you not stop making crooked the straight paths of the Lord? And now, behold, the hand of the Lord is upon you, and you will be blind and unable to see the sun for a time." Immediately mist and darkness fell upon him, and he went about seeking people to lead him by the hand. Then the proconsul believed, when he saw what had occurred, for he was astonished at the teaching of the Lord.
> -Acts 13:7-12

Here is what we see from this passage: Sergius Paulus was seeking to hear the Word of the Lord for himself. He was not yet convinced of the truth of it, merely curious about it. Elymas (who was first identified as Bar-Jesus, meaning Son of Jesus) was part of the proconsul. We are not told what experience, if any, he had with The Way (as the early Christians were called), only that he heavily opposed them. This was the work of Satan, for he was attempting to hinder a hungry soul from hearing the truth of the Gospel. Paul not only perceived that this man was under the influence of a demonic spirit, but through the Discerning of Spirits he was able to identify the exact spirits at work in this man. He identified him as being led by the spirits of deceit and villainy. This word "villainy" is "rhadiourgia," which can refer to mischief or the love of a lazy, effeminate lifestyle. Effeminate refers to that which is feminine, woman-like, or unmanly. We know that this contradicts God's divine order.

Kingdom Progression

What we come to understand, then, is that Paul, through the Discerning of Spirits, identified the spirits of deceit and perversion leading this man.

> As we were going to the place of prayer, we were met by a slave girl who had a spirit of divination and brought her owners much gain by fortune-telling. She followed Paul and us, crying out, "These men are servants of the Most High God, who proclaim to you the way of salvation." And this she kept doing for many days. Paul, having become greatly annoyed, turned and said to the spirit, "I command you in the name of Jesus Christ to come out of her." And it came out that very hour.
> -Acts 16:16-18

Immediately from the start of this passage we see that this woman was possessed by a spirit of divination. Whether it was Paul (who was used to identify such), Silas, or another present for this event. The who does not matter. Divination is the evil twin of prophecy, so to speak. On the outside, they appear very similar, but the key difference is the motivation behind such. Divination is most often motivated by selfishness, or greed, as we see from this passage. The owners of this woman took advantage of the spirit that had possessed her and were profiting from such.

Notice from both events what the result was. God did not give the individuals this gift just so they could know, a sort of "fun fact." God gives these gifts for a purpose. In the first example, we see that the Discerning of Spirits led to the power over those demonic spirits, which resulted in the belief of the proconsul. In the second example, though it ultimately led to Paul and Silas' imprisonment, it brought freedom and liberty to the poor girl who was subjected to mental, emotional, and spiritual abuse due to the greed of her owners. The Discerning of Spirits is not simply a cool trick. It is meant to be used in and for His Kingdom for the furthering of such.

Divers Kinds of Tongues and Interpretation of Tongues

Throughout the New Testament, we see a few different mentions of "tongues." These different aspects of tongues are often misunderstood as the same event, but such is not the case. If we examine Scripture closely, we discover that there are three primary variations of tongues. The first we see is speaking in tongues as the initial sign of one being filled with His Spirit. We talked about this at the beginning of the book when speaking on His Kingdom, specifically on how one enters His Kingdom. We discussed how this is through the New Birth which involves Spirit baptism which is always accompanied by the outward sign of speaking in tongues (see Acts 2:1-4; 10:44-48; 19:1-6).

The second aspect of tongues that we see mentioned throughout Scripture is that of praying in tongues post-New Birth experience. Paul tells us in Romans 8:26 that there are times when we know we need to pray, but we are lost on what to pray. We see the need but have no words. Paul tells us that in these times if we have first experienced the New Birth, His Spirit will intercede on our behalf and pray the prayer we do not know how to pray. He words it as "groans too deep for words," meaning it is an experience beyond what can be defined on a natural level. This implies that it is the supernatural event of speaking in tongues. Jude also told us, "But you, beloved, building yourselves up in your most holy faith and praying in the Holy Spirit" (Jude 1:20). We see, then, that praying in the Spirit not only prays the prayers we don't know how to pray, but it also edifies us. We are made stronger when we pray in tongues. This is also

Kingdom Progression

confirmed in I Corinthians 14:4-5.

The third aspect of tongues is what Paul was specifically referring to in this list of the Gifts of the Spirit. All who are born into the Kingdom of God must have spoken in tongues; furthermore, Paul and Jude admonish us all to pray in tongues. We understand, then, that these two aspects of tongues are not unique for certain situations but are meant for all to experience. Therefore, this third aspect is tongues given amid the congregation and is meant as a supernatural word for the body of believers (we will explain this momentarily). We often group together this Gift of the Spirit and the last mentioned by Paul (Interpretation of Tongues) into one, calling it tongues and interpretation of tongues. However, these are two distinct gifts. One may operate in both, thereby giving the message in tongues and the interpretation of such. However, what is normally seen, from my experience at least, is that there is one who gives the message in tongues, and then another gives the interpretation. I combined these two gifts not to say that they are the same, as stated above they are not the same, but because they do go hand-in-hand. They are difficult to separate. For where there is one, there ought to be the other. While they are not one gift, they are eternally interwoven.

The reason Paul stated that it was the Gift of Divers Kinds of Tongues is that there is not one specific tongue (language) in which one speaks. Paul stated that one can speak in the language of men (stated in the plural form, meaning that it could be any human language) or of angels (also in the plural, meaning there are various heavenly languages [see I Corinthians 13:1]). After the message in tongues has been given, then there is the interpretation. This word in Greek is "hermēneia" which can mean interpretation or explanation. The Webster's Dictionary defines interpretation in two different ways that could be used to better understand this gift: "explanation of unintelligible words in a language that is intelligible," or "the act of expounding or unfolding what is not understood or not obvious."

Understanding such, we would define these two gifts in operation with one another as God supernaturally, yet verbally, speaking to His people a precise word.

If one examines the Book of Acts, there are no accounts recorded by Luke of this gift in operation. Thankfully, Paul does provide us with crucial teaching regarding this gift that ought to be examined.

First, Paul made this statement: "So with yourselves, since you are eager for manifestations of the Spirit, strive to excel in building up the church. Therefore, one who speaks in a tongue should pray that he may interpret" (I Corinthians 14:12-13). We see that Paul first establishes that each Gift of the Spirit is for "building up the church." He then says, "therefore," meaning that the statement he is about to make is directly connected to the one just made. The statement to follow tells us that where there is a public utterance of tongues, there ought to be interpretation. Paul admonished that the one who spoke in tongues should pray for the interpretation. As I said before, this does not always mean that the one who gives the initial message will also interpret it. Even so, one should still pray for the interpretation in case no one else receives such.

Second, Paul said later in the same chapter, "If any speak in a tongue, let there be only two or at most three, and each in turn, and let someone interpret. But if there is no one to interpret, let each of them keep silent in church and speak to himself and to God" (I Corinthians 14:27-28). Some misinterpret this statement to indicate that people shouldn't speak in tongues at all unless there is an interpretation. Again, that is to misunderstand the three different aspects of speaking in tongues. For Paul stated, referencing back to I Corinthians 14:4-5, that he desired that all would speak in tongues (and this referred to the personal aspect of such). What Paul was referring to in I Corinthians 14:27-28 was the proper order in which the Gifts of Divers Kinds of Tongues

Kingdom Progression

and Interpretation of Tongues ought to be followed in a church service. First, he starts by saying that there can be anywhere from one to (at the most) three messages in tongues given. If these messages in tongues are truly from God, they will not overlap but will all be given in turn. However, even though there may be one to three messages in tongues given, there is only one interpretation. This may confuse some: Why three messages but one interpretation? Is there not some of the message that we are missing then? Not necessarily. Think about a foreign language compared to your native language. Let's use English for example compared to another language. There have been times in multicultural services when I have heard the minister speak in English a particular sentence and then pause to allow the interpreters to speak. Oftentimes, what the interpreters say is two to three times as long as the English sentence. This does not mean the interpreter changed what was said, it simply points to the fact that the languages are not the same. They don't have the same words or length of words or structure of words or alphabet. We really can't take two different languages and expect them to line up. This is why there can be one to three messages in tongues given but only one interpretation.

Paul continues to say that if no interpretation is given, then those who spoke the message in tongues should remain silent. What Paul was conveying to us was that if no interpretation comes forth, the one who spoke the message in tongues should not keep on repeating the message in tongues. There could be several reasons for there being no interpretation. One, it could be that the one who initially spoke the message in tongues misunderstood. As we discussed, one aspect of tongues is personal, between the individual and God. It could be that God was trying to do a work in the individual, but they thought it was for the body of believers. It could also be the message in tongues was truly for the body, but the one to whom the interpretation was given lacked faith to speak what God was speaking to them. Regardless of the exact reason, repeating the message in tongues is not going to benefit any apart from the interpretation. For Paul states in I Corinthians 14:5 that tongues (in regard to this Gift of the Spirit) is of no benefit to the Church if there is no interpretation thereof.

We see, then, how crucial both gifts are to the body but only when they work together in order and unity. These two gifts are often looked at as very strange, far more than any other gift. This is due to how unlike they are compared to anything in the natural realm. Regardless of how "strange" these gifts may seem, we cannot forsake them. We ought to pursue them just as heartily as we do any other gift. These gifts are crucial to the Church, for it is God's direct word to His people.

Operating in the Gifts of the Spirit

In the chapter following Paul's list of the Gifts of the Spirit, Paul gives us vital teaching on how we ought to operate in each gift. As he said at the close of chapter twelve, "but earnestly desire the higher gifts. And I will show you a still more excellent way" (I Corinthians 12:31). We examined the first portion of this Scripture, how it more accurately states that we are to earnestly desire the gift that is needed for that specific moment. Then he states there is a "more excellent way" to do such. "Excellent" is "huperbolē," and "way" is "hodos." One way this could be translated is "a far better course of conduct." Paul is informing us that there is a particular way to operate in the Gifts of the Spirit that far exceeds any other manner. What is this "a far better course of conduct"?

> If I speak in the tongues of men and of angels, but have not love, I am a noisy gong or a clanging cymbal. And if I have prophetic powers, and understand all mysteries and all

knowledge, and if I have all faith, so as to remove mountains, but have not love, I am nothing. If I give away all I have, and if I deliver up my body to be burned, but have not love, I gain nothing. Love is patient and kind; love does not envy or boast; it is not arrogant or rude. It does not insist on its own way; it is not irritable or resentful; it does not rejoice at wrongdoing, but rejoices with the truth. Love bears all things, believes all things, hopes all things, endures all things. Love never ends. As for prophecies, they will pass away; as for tongues, they will cease; as for knowledge, it will pass away...So now faith, hope, and love abide, these three; but the greatest of these is love.
-I Corinthians 13:1-8,13

We will look at again at verses 1-3 of this passage in the final chapter of this book, but we must examine it here as well as it is integral to operating in the Gifts of the Spirit. When we examine love in the final chapter, The Call to All, we will examine it more so in regard to how it is conveyed toward others. Here, our focus is going to look at love as Paul so beautifully defined it.

To begin his discourse on the "a far better course of conduct," Paul begins by drawing attention to several, but not all, of the Gifts of the Spirit. He specifically names, Divers Kinds of Tongues, Gift of Prophecy, Word of Wisdom, Word of Knowledge, and Gift of Faith. Just because he did not name the other gifts does not exclude them from his statement in this passage. Simply by him mentioning some of the gifts, it thereby may well encompass all the gifts. We know this because it is the same Spirit, Lord, and God who empowers every Gift of the Spirit, so they are all connected to the One (see I Corinthians 12:4-6). What is the statement that he makes regarding the Gifts of the Spirit? Simply, if love is not the driving force behind such, the one attempting to operate in such is annoying (a noisy gong or a clanging cymbal) and becomes nothing because of it (implying that even if they had something before, it was now lost). Paul then takes it a step beyond just operating in the Gifts of the Spirit and names two major things that we as Born Again believers are encouraged to do: that is, give with generosity and live sacrificially. Paul states that if love is not the driving force behind these, then the one who does such gains nothing. Or in other words, they reap no eternal rewards by doing so. God typically praises and exalts one who would willingly do such things, but God looks beyond the outward and peers into the inward: one's motivations (see I Samuel 16:7; Matthew 15:7-9).

Love must be the sincere motivation behind all that we do for the Kingdom of God, not just regarding the Gifts of the Spirit. The question we are then forced to ask ourselves is, what is love? What are the characteristics of love? Thankfully, Paul broke that down for us. Paul informs us that love is patient and kind, does not envy or boast, is not arrogant or rude, does not insist on its own way, is not irritable or resentful, and does not rejoice in wrongdoing but rejoices in the truth.

Let's examine each of these characteristics. First, we see patient. "Patient" is "makrothumeō," and it means "to not lose heart; to persevere patiently and bravely in enduring misfortunes and troubles; to be patient in bearing the offenses and injuries of others." Here, then, are three distinct qualities of the patience of love: it does not give up; it is strong and brave, even in the face of chaos; and it does not hold others hostage by hanging their failures over their heads. This last aspect of patience is particularly catching, for we have examined the importance of forgiveness at the start of this chapter. We think that by not forgiving, that we are hurting them (this alone is the opposite of the nature of love), but in

Kingdom Progression

actuality, we hurt ourselves. For by not forgiving, we will not be forgiven (see Matthew 6:14-15).

The second characteristic is kind. This is "chrēsteuomai." What is interesting about this word is that it has a little bit of variety when it comes to its meaning. It can mean kind, gentle, or even mild. However, it can also mean, "to show oneself useful." This is very interesting, for we see, then, that to be kind is more than simply being nice, it is also proving yourself trustworthy by your actions. A phrase I have heard more times than I can count is "People don't care how much you know until they know how much you care." Empty words mean nothing, so what do your actions say? Does the way you act convey love?

Next, we see that love does not envy. "Envy" is "zēloō," which is a complex word, for it has both good and bad meanings attached to it. We see that this word can mean things such as zealous, fervent, or intentional. All good aspects when used appropriately. The flip side to this word is "to be heated or to boil with envy, hatred, anger." This is the meaning that Paul was pointing to, hence the "not" before the "envy." Webster's Dictionary defines "envy" as "to feel uneasiness, mortification or discontent, at the sight of superior excellence, reputation or happiness enjoyed by another." What Paul is describing here is one who is utterly consumed by such a mentality and attitude. Meaning, envy is not a simple hint of jealousy, wishing you had what another has. Rather, the one who envies doesn't care about having what another has, they simply don't want the other person to have it.

The fourth characteristic is that love does not boast. "Boast" is "perpereuomai," which means "a self-display, employing rhetorical embellishments in extolling one's self excessively." Meaning, this is one who only cares about self; thus, they only talk about self. This is the opposite of love, for love genuinely cares for and about those around them. Love attentively listens to others. Love knows when to speak and when to listen. This is not to say that to love, one must not care about themselves. This is an unhealthy idea surrounding what love is. The one who loves still cares for and about themselves, but they are willing to set themselves aside for a time to meet the needs of others that are more pressing.

Next, we see that love is not arrogant. This word is "phusioō," which can refer to either pride or vanity. We have extensively looked at pride previously and have seen how it has no place in His Kingdom. Here, then, let's focus briefly on vanity. "Vanity," according to Webster's Dictionary, means "emptiness; want of substance to satisfy desire." There are several definitions of vanity, but they all echo the same truth: one who is vain is truly empty. They recognize the emptiness in themselves, but instead of filling that hole with things that will truly fill them up, they attempt to fill themselves with simple "substance." Meaning, filling themselves with things of this world: earthly, carnal, and temporal things. Things that hold no eternal value. The only things that fill the emptiness within us are God and His love.

The sixth characteristic is that love is not rude. "Rude" here is the Greek word "aschēmoneō." This word simply means "unbecoming." One way to define this word, according to Webster's Dictionary, is "improper for the person or character." Meaning, this is a course of conduct that is contrary to what is expected of the individual due to who they are, or at least, who they claim to be. When people hear that an individual is a Christian, there is automatically a particular conduct that they expect to experience from them. The true state of one's Christianity (in other words, the true state of their relationship with Jesus [the level of love they walk in]) can be easily assessed based on their conduct.

The phrase "Does not insist on its own way" consists of several words in Greek: "zēteō ou heautou." This refers to one who is willing to acknowledge that their will, their desires, and their plans are not the only ones that matter.

Kingdom Progression

There are others involved in every situation, and how they think and feel about a given situation matters just as much as the way you do. Of course, this phrase also implies an acknowledgment that God's will is supreme, and He knows best. This phrase implies a willingness to lay oneself aside.

Next, we see that love is not irritated. This is "paroxunō," and it can mean "easily provoked," or "to stir up." This word, then, carries a double-edged meaning. By Paul using this word, he was stating that one dwelling in love, first, is not hot headed. One who is not immediately reactive to situations, responding based on assumption. Two, neither does this one stir up those around them. This, in essence, describes one who walks in peace (referring to the opposite of what this word means, as Paul said, "not irritated"). True peace will affect both the individual and their environment.

Eighth, we see another phrase: "logizomai ou kakos." This phrase refers to one who does not plot revenge. Or one who does not seek to "get back" at another. We saw how an aspect of patience is forgiveness. Well, true forgiveness lets go. If you are still holding on to a situation, thinking of what could happen to the other individual, and then you would feel good, you have not yet forgiven them. Love forgives and forgets. Love lets the past stay in the past.

The final characteristics of love mentioned by Paul we will look at as one, for they truly go hand-in-hand. First, we see that we are to "rejoice," but then we see that we are "not to rejoice." Webster's Dictionary defines "rejoice" as "to experience joy and gladness in a high degree; to be exhilarated with lively and pleasurable sensations; to exult." Therefore, we do not become exhilarated over "wrongdoing." This is "adikia," and it can simply be defined as "unrighteousness." Rather, we are to be exhilarated by "truth." What is the truth though? It seems everyone has their ideas as to what is true and not true. Good and evil. How do we know what to rejoice over and what not to? In John 16:13, Jesus described the Holy Spirit as the "Spirit of truth." Meaning, all things about God and His work in us and through us, and around us, are truth. That is what we rejoice over. The work of the Lord Jesus.

Paul continues after this list of characteristics by listing four states of being that love is eternally dwelling in: bearing all things, believing all things, hoping all things, and enduring all things.

First, we see that love bears. "Bears" is "stegō," and it refers to protecting another from threat or harm. Meaning, the one who loves is willing to stand in the line of fire for the sake of another. Love is sacrificial. Love is courageous. Love is strong. Jesus said the greatest display of love that one could give to another is to lay down their life for them (see John 15:13). All of this is encompassed in this state of bearing all things.

Next, we see that love believes. "Believes" is "pisteuō." One way to define this word is "to be persuaded of; to have confidence in." Along with belief, this word is often translated as faith. I find these two definitions particularly interesting: "to be persuaded of" and "to have confidence in." Lack of trust is something that we see rampaging through our society. Everyone is skeptical of everyone, and no one takes anyone's word for anything. One says a thing to another and they say, "I believe you, but…" That statement shows a lack of belief though. The reason for the lack of trust in our society is the lack of love. Love says, "I'm going to put my faith in you and show you that I trust you by leaving this in your hands."

Third, is that love hopes. We have looked at hope previously—when defining faith—in the second chapter. What we discussed was that biblical hope truly means expectation. Therefore, love is full of expectation. "Elpizō" here can be translated as just that: "to expect." Expectation is present when something you believe, or have faith in, has so totally gripped you that no matter what your circumstances may tell you, you still expect to see it come to pass.

Kingdom Progression

Finally, we see that love endures. This is truly a beautiful picture. This word is "hypomenō" and one way to define it is "to remain or stay behind when others have departed." What we see, then, is that love is faithful, constant, true, and eternal. Love never fails. Love doesn't give up. When all else has failed, love never will. When everyone and everything else has given up, love will remain. Love can always be counted on. Paul affirms this truth in the very next verse. He begins by stating that "love never ends." He then goes on to name three Gifts of the Spirit: Gift of Prophecy, Divers Kinds of Tongues, and Word of Knowledge, and he states that there will come a day when these shall end. This day is the day of His return, for these gifts are only present in the Church to prepare His Body for His return. When He then returns, what need will we have for them? We will be with Him. The Gifts of the Spirit and the Five-Fold Ministry will one day cease to be needed, but on that day, love will remain. Love will always be. For God is love (see I John 4:8,16).

One final statement on love that Paul makes is that at the end of the day, three things remain: faith, hope, and love, but the greatest is love. Here are the three fundamental things that make up the entirety of a child of God. We have already examined all three of these, so we will not do so again. However, to repeat for sake of clarity, faith is the foundation that we stand upon. Without it, there can be no relationship with God. Hope is expectation. Hope looks to the future not with mere optimism, but with such a conviction that all will come to pass. Hope is full of joy and patience: joy amid struggle, for you know the victory is on the other side, and patience to see it through. Love will always triumph over all, for He is the very essence of love. Love is Him. Love must be at the very center of all that we do, or else all that we do is in vain.

Conclusion

We have looked at much in this chapter, discussing several topics: finding our place in the Body, the Gifts of service, the Gifts of the Spirit, and love being the catalyst. All of this is essential to understanding the call of God on our lives. Too often we shrug off important things, thinking that we will somehow simply figure it out along the way. This is a dangerous mindset, for it can lead to self-deception. You can become so confident in what you are doing that you think it's right, yet all along it has been wrong. We mistake confidence for truth. They are not the same. We can be confident in truth, and ought to be. However, we can also be confident in deception. We must understand the Gifts that God has given so that we don't abuse and misuse them. How do we ensure that we do not do so? By keeping love at the center of everything. Again, we must properly understand love. We dare not have our definition of love but operate apart from such. This will lead us to deception. In all that we do for God, we must do it according to His plan, His truth. We need to understand His ways. Only in doing such will we operate in the manner in which He desires.

5
The Five-Fold Ministry

The Five-Fold Ministry is a vital aspect of the prosperity of the Church. Unfortunately, it has been widely misunderstood for some time. When something is misunderstood, one of two things happen: one, it is either misused or abused; or two, it is utterly discarded. What we do not understand, though, is that without these crucial offices in operation, the Church cannot become what it was designed to be. What I aim to do here, then, at the start, is to define the role of the Five-Fold Ministry and its purpose as a whole. Then once we have defined the overall purpose of the Five-Fold Ministry, we will then examine each one individually.

The Role and Purpose of the Five-Fold Ministry
Defining the Five-Fold Ministry

> And he gave the apostles, the prophets, the evangelists, the shepherds and teachers.
> -Ephesians 4:11

After Paul gives the list of the Five-Fold Ministry, Paul then goes on to say this:

> To equip the saints for the work of ministry, for building up the body of Christ, until we all attain to the unity of the faith and of the knowledge of the Son of God, to mature manhood, to the measure of the stature of the fullness of Christ, so that we may no longer

> be children, tossed to and fro by the waves and carried about by every wind of doctrine, by human cunning, by craftiness in deceitful schemes.
> -Ephesians 4:12-14

We will break this down and examine this passage of Scripture in depth momentarily, but what is seen from the simple examination is that the Five-Fold Ministry operates in a place of leadership in the Church. Toward the beginning of this book, I mentioned that every kingdom has a government and that the purpose of the government is to help the ruler of the kingdom to rule according to the ruler's will. The Kingdom of God works in the same manner. God is the divine ruler over all, but He placed a government within His Body, the Church, to help Him lead His Church according to His will. A simple way to define the Five-Fold Ministry, then, is the government of God placed within His Church.

There is a model that I have seen multiple times, and I am not sure who created this model, but it conveys the purpose of the Five-Fold Ministry simply. First, there is an extended hand with its fingers all stretched out. This hand represents the hand of God. On each finger and the thumb is listed an Office of the Five-Fold Ministry and its role. For simplicities sake, each role attributed to each office begins with the letter "g."

This is the layout we see:

-Thumb: the Apostle, govern
-Pointer Finger: the Prophet, guide
-Center Finger: the Evangelist, gather
-Ring Finger: the Shepherd (Pastor), guard
-Pinky Finger: the Teacher, ground

In Scripture, the hand (most times the right hand, but the hand in general) represents authority, power, and

Kingdom Progression

active work (see Exodus 15:6,12; Psalms 138:7). What this model is conveying to us, then, is that the Five-Fold Ministry operates as God's authority in the Church. One thing that my Pastor said once was, "No one has the right to correct the Church except the Five-Fold Ministry."

Something important to understand is that the Five-Fold Ministry does not sit at a place of special privilege above all others. You do not have to be something special, or extremely talented, to be in such a position. All who are called by God are called according to His will, and His plan, not according to the individual's level of "special-ness." We've examined the question, Can God Trust You? We've examined how there are aspects of an individual's level of devotion (private and corporate) that God looks at, but He is not biased. As the Bible says, He is no respecter of persons. Meaning, He shows no partiality to one group of people over another. Or, to one type of personality over another (see Acts 10:24-25; Romans 2:1; and James 2:1). Anyone can be called to the Five-Fold Ministry so long as they align with His standard of devotion. However, it is important to understand that not all are called to the Five-Fold Ministry. If all operated in the government, who would be governed? God has selected "some," as Ephesians 4:11 (KJV) says, to fill these Offices.

Again, those who are called to these Offices should not think more highly of themselves than they ought to. Those of us who are called are no better than those who aren't. The only difference between us is the call of God on our lives. We talked about what ministry is, and one of the things mentioned was servanthood. No matter the position, no matter the office, we are servants first and foremost. Jesus said, "So the last will be first, and the first last" (Matthew 20:16). Also, "And he said to them, 'The kings of the Gentiles exercise lordship over them, and those in authority over them are called benefactors. But not so with you. Rather, let the greatest among you become as the youngest, and the leader as one who serves. For who is the greater, one who reclines at table or one who serves? Is it not the one who reclines at table? But I am among you as the one who serves'" (Luke 22:25-27). What we see is that the greater level at which one operates for God, the greater the servant they are to become. Jesus accurately conveyed how in the kingdoms of the world, the greater the level one achieves, the more they are served. However, the Kingdom of God operates opposite the world, for Jesus is the greatest of all, yet, He came as a servant, so are we to do.

It is important to stress these things because we tend to get stuck in our heads and become prideful. It is crucial that no matter the position or office God may call us to, we operate out of humility. Servanthood is key to ministry. As the Five-Fold Ministry, we may be God's chosen leaders of His people, but we lead them by serving them.

Function of the Five-Fold Ministry

What exactly does the Five-Fold Ministry do? Paul begins by saying that they "equip the saints for the work of ministry." "Equip" is "katartismos," and it means "completely furnished, equipped, perfected." Perfect, as it is used in this verse, refers to having everything necessary. What we see is the saints being equipped for "the work of ministry." Another way to translate this would be "the labor of service." Every saint of God, every member of the Body, has a ministry. All are called to serve. The Five-Fold Ministry's job is to help the Body in two ways: one, discover the ministry God has called them to, and two, be prepared to operate in that ministry. This has several different parts. For there is a foundational level that the Five-Fold Ministry helps the Body come to that will enable them to step into their ministry. However, the foundation is just the beginning. The Five-Fold Ministry will then continue to equip the Body beyond the fundamental aspects to enable them to grow in

Kingdom Progression

their ministry.

This is why Paul continued by saying that their purpose is for the "building up of the Body of Christ." "Building up" here is "oikodomē." This word points to the act of constructing a building upon the already laid foundation. The Five-Fold Ministry does not lay the foundation and then say, "Good luck, see you later." Once the foundation has been laid, their job has just begun. For they are then to help ensure that the proper building is constructed upon that foundation. What good is a concrete slab laid as a foundation, with no structure atop it? The foundation only fulfills its purpose when it properly upholds its structure. We cannot overlook the necessity of the foundation, for without a proper foundation, the structure would fall. Both elements are crucial and cannot be forsaken. Many want to jump in and learn all they can as fast as they can. That is fantastic. However, the Five-Fold Ministry's job is to ensure that they are fed the foundational truths first so that they have something to build upon. What good is it to teach one about the Gifts of the Spirit if they do not understand the New Birth? There is a proper order to truth being conveyed, and part of the Five-Fold Ministry's job is to ensure that the order is followed.

Duration of the Five-Fold Ministry

Following what the Five-Fold Ministry was given by God to do, Paul then conveys to us the duration of the offices they operate in. This is made evident by the word "until." We must be careful though, for many misread this and assume that the time for the Five-Fold Ministry has ended, thinking they were only in place for a short time. Paul gives us details of this "until" and that is when "we all attain to the unity of the faith and of the knowledge of the Son of God, to mature manhood, to the measure of the stature of the fullness of Christ."

The first "until" marker is attaining the "unity of the faith." "Attain" is "katantaō," which can be translated "to arrive at." Meaning, this is a moment, a place reached. It is specific. It is not an "I think I've 'arrived.'" It is a true arrival, without a doubt, without question. "Unity" is "henotēs" which can mean "unity" or "oneness." "Oneness" properly conveys the true definition of what unity means. As Acts 2:1-4 indicates, they were of "one mind and one accord" (KJV). Meaning, there is not my opinion and then your opinion; rather, there is only His opinion (the truth) and us coming into alignment with Him in complete agreement.

"The" is extremely significant, for it points to something specific. If Paul were to simply say, "Until we all attain unity of faith," this would be extremely vague. Faith can mean a variety of things. By him putting "the" in front of "faith," he was pinpointing something specific. What was the specific thing which he was pointing to? "Faith," which is "pistis." This word can also be understood as doctrine. "Doctrine" refers to the truth of the Bible. What Paul was then conveying was that there are many "doctrines" (definitions of truth) in the world, but there is one "the doctrine." One specific truth (see Galatians 1:6-9).

What Paul conveys to us is that the Five-Fold Ministry will be in operation until we arrive at a place of complete and total agreement with the specific truth that God has laid out in His Word.

There is a second half we see to this first "until" marker, which is attaining "the knowledge of the Son of God." The main word that bears examination is "knowledge." We've already looked at "attain" and "the" and we know that the "Son of God" is in reference to Jesus. Therefore, this first portion we can readily define as, "arriving at something specific" ("attain" and "the"). What is "knowledge" then? This is "epignōsis" and can be defined as "precise and correct knowledge." Meaning, this is not simply something partially understood. This is a complete understanding. No questions,

Kingdom Progression

unknowns, or mysteries. Everything revealed. Additionally, this thing that is fully revealed is Jesus.

Before continuing to the other "until" markers, we can already see what is transpiring. These things mentioned by Paul will not be truly "attained" by us "until" we are taken up into glory to be with Him for eternity. Meaning, the Five-Fold Ministry will be active in His Church until the day of His return. There have been some who have thought that the day and age for Apostles and Prophets has ended, and it is only the Evangelists, Pastors, and Teachers at work in the Church. Nowhere in Scripture does it indicate to us that there will ever be a day when some of the offices will be in operation, while others are not. All will be in complete operation until we are with Him in glory.

The third "until" marker is "mature manhood." "Mature" is "teleios," and it means "brought to completion," while "manhood" is "anēr" which simply refers to one fully developed in age and stature, as opposed to a child, or youth. In essence, Paul is making a double statement for emphasis. He is stating that the Five-Fold Ministry will be in operation until we attain the complete definition of maturity. One way that the Bible often defines maturity is "perfection." In other words, "brought to complete perfection." We again see how this will not be experienced until we arrive at Perfection (capitalized due to referring to Heaven and His presence). True perfection does not exist in this world, for perfection cannot abide with sin.

The final "until" is "to the measure of the stature of the fullness of Christ." "Measure" is "metron" which refers to a specific measurement of something. "Stature" is "hēlikia" which refers to one's whole life. What is seen, then, is that there is a specific amount of a specific life we are to attain. What is the specific amount of the specific life? Paul answers this question: "the fullness of Christ." Meaning, this final "until" marker is when He has been completely formed in us. Where no ounce of our fleshly, carnal being exists any longer. Where no sin has even a chance of pulling us down. Where it is only Him. Again, this is something that will not be achieved until we are transformed in the sky with Him and receive our glorious bodies (see Philippians 3:20-21; I Thessalonians 4:16-17).

The idea that the Five-Fold Ministry is no longer in operation, or is only partially in operation, is absurd and contradicts the teachings of Scripture. The only way such has been withheld is if we were the ones to do so. God has not taken away His government. His Church is still on this earth, meaning those He appointed to lead His Church are still in operation. We must allow God to manifest His designed order for the Church if we are going to see it thrive as He desires it to. All of Asia Minor heard the Gospel in the span of just two years (see Acts 19:10). This transpired out of the Church of Ephesus, the very Church Paul was instructing regarding the Five-Fold Ministry. Could it be that they were so effective in reaching their world because they had fully grasped the designed order of God?

The Offices

Now that we have defined the role of the Five-Fold Ministry as a whole (to lead the Church and to edify such unto growth), and the duration thereof (until His return), we can now begin to dive into the individual offices within the Five-Fold Ministry. Again, this is the Apostle, Prophet, Evangelist, Pastor, and Teacher.

> And he gave the apostles, the prophets, the evangelists, the shepherds and teachers.
> -Ephesians 4:11

There is something I want to mention before diving into this; some have the mindset that the Teacher is not its own office, but a leg off of the Pastor (Shepherd). They have

Kingdom Progression

this mind due to two lines of thought: one, Paul did not put the word "some" (KJV) before mentioning the office of the Teacher as he did with the others, and two, Pastors ought to be able-bodied teachers. My aim for mentioning this is not to talk down about any but to draw attention to different thoughts individuals have.

Here in this study, I will be examining the office of the Teacher as a separate office apart from that of the Pastor. Here is my reasoning for addressing the thought that Pastors ought to be able-bodied teachers: anyone operating in any office or ministry, or any mature Christian, ought to be an able-bodied teacher. The idea that Pastors alone ought to be such does not seem to me as the correct train of thought. As mentioned when addressing the character of one whom God trusts, we mentioned that they ought to be "able to teach." Being able to teach someone differs from operating in the office of the Teacher within the Five-Fold Ministry.

The second point demonstrating that the Teacher is separate from the Pastor comes from the Book of Acts: "Now there were in the church at Antioch prophets and teachers, Barnabas, Simeon who was called Niger, Lucius of Cyrene, Manaen a lifelong friend of Herod the tetrarch, and Saul" (Acts 13:1). Luke here specifically mentioned two offices present, that of the Prophet and Teacher. He did not mention any Pastors present, though. Again, this implies that it is a separate Office.

The final point I will make to demonstrate why I believe the Teacher to be a separate office comes from the words of Paul to Timothy: "for which I was appointed a preacher and apostle and teacher" (II Timothy 1:11). The Greek word used for the office of the Pastor in Ephesians 4:11 is "poimēn," referring to a shepherd, one who watches over a flock, or a guardian. The Greek word for "preacher" here is "kēryx," a completely different word simply meaning, "a proclaimer, publisher, or preacher." Therefore, what we see is that Paul was stating that he operated within two, separate Five-Fold Ministry Offices: that of the Apostle and that of the Teacher. Again, nowhere do we see the office of the Pastor mentioned. It is for these reasons, as stated, that I believe the Teacher to be its own office. This being the case, I will be examining it as such.

Again, I do not say these things to attempt to belittle those who think otherwise. I say these things simply to express my understanding of such and to explain why I think in the manner that I do.

One final thing before moving on: it's important to understand that not all the offices operate at the same capacity or level. This is not to say that some offices are inferior to others. For every office is integral to the function of His government. However, each Office differs, for if they were all the same, just reiterations of each other, what would be the point for there being five? A simple manner in which my Pastor described it, that has stuck with me, is that as you go down the list of the offices, they become more focused. He defined it as such: the Apostles operate on a global level, the Prophets on a national level, the Evangelists on a cultural level, the Pastors on a congregational level, and the Teachers on an individual level. This is not an exact way to describe the operation of these offices, for there is always variation. To give an example, regarding the Apostle, my Pastor says that there can be "Horizontal Apostles" (globally focused) and "Vertical Apostles" (locally focused). Regardless, the ministry of the Apostle is the same. This breakdown merely provides us with a rudimentary level of understanding regarding these offices' operations.

This is vital to understand because when one called to the Five-Fold Ministry discovers their office in such, they need to understand what their focus is. If a Teacher tried to operate on a worldwide level, they would be out of alignment and not operate in the capacity which God designed. Their intentions may be good, thinking that they are trying to expand their reach. However, good intentions

Kingdom Progression

do not override the divine plan and will of God.

In all that we do for Him, we need to ensure that we walk humbly according to what He desires. As the Prophet Micah stated, "He has told you, O man, what is good; and what does the LORD require of you but to do justice, and to love kindness, and to walk humbly with your God" (Micah 6:8)?

The Apostle: Governs

"And he gave the apostles…"(Ephesians 4:11).

To begin our study of the office of the Apostle, let's go back to the hand model. We mentioned how the Apostle is represented by the thumb. Something very interesting is seen from this: an individual can easily take their thumb and move it to perfectly touch the tip of each finger, but no other finger can do such. What this model immediately conveys to us, then, is the office of the Apostle spans all five Offices within the Five-Fold Ministry. This makes sense when we look back to the simplified definition of the Apostle's role: to govern.

The Apostles are often the ones first sent into a new area: they establish. This being the case, they need to have the reach and level of operation of all five offices to effectively reach the new area.

When we look at the Apostles of the New Testament, we see this truth displayed. We already mentioned how Paul declared that he operated within the offices of the Apostle and the Teacher. Also, we quoted Acts 13:1 to demonstrate that the Teacher was recognized as a separate office. In that Scripture, we see several individuals mentioned as operating within the offices of the Prophet and the Teacher: Barnabas, Simeon, Lucius, Manaen, and Saul (Paul). Therefore, Paul also operated within the office of the Prophet. Also, in regard to Paul, looking back to II Timothy 11:1, we examined the word "preacher." I examined it in a way to demonstrate that it is not the same as a Pastor, because in our culture the terms "preacher" and "pastor" are often used inseparably, but they truly are two different functions. In examining this word, "kēryx," we stated how it means "a proclaimer, publisher, or preacher." This could point to Paul identifying that he also operated in the office of the Evangelist. In Acts 8:5 we see Philip who was later identified as operating in the office of the Evangelist (see Acts 21:8). Acts 8:5 states that Philip "proclaimed." This is "kērysso" which comes from the same root as "kēryx," and it also carries the same meaning. Thus, we surmise that the operation of the Evangelist is defined as proclaiming, or publishing, which is what Paul stated he also did. We, therefore, see that Paul for sure operated in three of the five offices (Apostle, Prophet, and Teacher) and most likely the Evangelist as well. The only office that is not directly linked to Paul in Scripture is that of the Pastor.

If we look at the Apostle Peter (more of a "Vertical Apostle") as an example though, we do see that he operated within the office of the Pastor. One thing to note, which I will dive into more when we truly examine the Pastoral Office, is that the word for "pastors" in Ephesians 4:11 is better translated as "shepherds." For clarity's sake, using the wording that would be best identifiable by the reader, I chose to use "Pastor," but on a personal level I prefer to use "Shepherd."

Peter stated this: "So I exhort the elders among you, as a fellow elder and a witness of the sufferings of Christ, as well as a partaker in the glory that is going to be revealed: shepherd the flock of God that is among you, exercising oversight, not under compulsion, but willingly, as God would have you; not for shameful gain, but eagerly" (I Peter 5:1-2).

Peter wrote here to the elders, and then explicitly identified himself as a fellow elder. He then goes on to convey the role of the elder, "shepherd the flock of God." We read this passage by Peter and think he is referring to a

Kingdom Progression

function separate from that of a Pastor, but by his definition thereof, we see that he was referring to the office of the Pastor. Moreover, he stated that he was a fellow one among them.

What we see, then, is that just because an Apostle can span across all five offices does not mean they do. Not every ministry is going to look the same, for we are all unique and operate within a unique call of God. If we examine the ministry of Peter, we see that he was called more so to operate as an Apostle and Pastor, as we have examined. For he was the first leader of the Church. He stood up and spoke on behalf of the other Apostles present on the Day of Pentecost (see Acts 2:14), and he operated in a seat of authority among the Church leaders during its early years (see Acts 15:6-11).

If we flip our attention to Paul (more of a "Horizontal Apostle"), we also see him operate as a leader of the Church, but on a much different scale. He operated more so in the field, for he was always on the move. Going from city to city. Establishing the works, and then moving on, then coming back around and building up those previously established works. We very clearly see then how the ministry of an Apostle could look different, depending on what exactly God called them to.

If we wanted another example, we could look to the Apostle John who operated powerfully in the office of the Prophet: simply look at the Book of Revelation for proof of such.

We are brought to the question: What exactly is an Apostle? The Greek word for "apostles" is "Apostolos," and it means "a delegate, ambassador, or commissioner." What do these words point to, though? The Webster's Dictionary defines these three words like so: delegate, "a person appointed and sent by another with powers to transact business as his representative;" ambassador, "a minister of the highest rank employed by one prince or state, at the court of another, to manage the public concerns of his own prince or state, and representing the power and dignity of his sovereign;" and commissioner, "a person who has a commission or warrant from the proper authority, to perform some office, or execute some business, for the person or government which employs him, and gives him authority." We see that these three words differ slightly in meaning but all represent the same idea. The understanding of an Apostle we gain by looking at these three words is that they are God's direct, highest authority active in His Church. They represent Him directly. They carry His total authority, and they carry out His direct will.

It is from these three definitions of "apostolos" (delegate, ambassador, and commissioner) and their accompanying definitions that we derive the simplified definition of the Apostle's role: to govern.

We gain further understanding of the office of the Apostle when we define the word, "govern." The Webster's Dictionary offers a few definitions of such that offer further insight.

One, "to direct and control, as the actions or conduct of men, either by established laws or by arbitrary will; to regulate by authority; to keep within the limits prescribed by law or sovereign will." What is seen from this first definition is that the Apostles establish and implement the Will and direction of God. Something crucially important to understand is that the Apostles do not decide for themselves what the direction of the Church is. Such an idea would put man in the seat of God. God alone has such sovereign authority over His Church. However, He uses His Apostles to voice His Will and direction for them. This means that God has given the Apostles greater insight and discernment in this area: knowing His Will. One must remember though that all that we do must be done through love, as we talked about. Therefore, when the Apostles hear from God and go to implement His divine Will, they do not do so in an authoritarian or tyrannical manner. They do so in love and in agreement with His nature (The Fruit of the Spirit, see

Kingdom Progression

Galatians 5:22-23).

Two, "to control; to restrain; to keep in due subjection; as, to govern the passions or temper." This is a very important one. The Apostles are not only used by God to implement His will in His Church, but they also keep the Church in line. Meaning, when the Church needs correction, the Apostles stand at the forefront of such. When the Church is beginning to get out of alignment, the Apostles remind them of the will of God. When the Church wants to be and act more like the world, it is the Apostle that stands up and reminds them of who they are children of. The world did not save them, it was the Lord.

Three, "to direct; to steer; to regulate the course or motion of a ship." This final definition brings into one thought the previous two definitions. The Apostles stand at the helm, so to speak, of the Church. Their job is to keep the Church on course in alignment with where God desires them. When the Church begins to steer away, the Apostles turn the ship back on course. The one who stands at the helm is in control of all other aspects of the ship. Every crew member listens to the voice of the one at the helm. In like fashion is the Apostle. It is as I said, the Five-Fold Ministry is the leadership of the Church, but the Apostles are the leaders of the Five-Fold Ministry.

I've already stated this, but I feel it bears repeating for emphasis sake. The Apostles do not sit in the seat of God, nor are their opinions on things divine direction. Those who operate in the office of the Apostle bear a much heavier weight, for they must ensure that they are completely submitted. Due to their office, they operate in a place, as I said, where they direct the Church. If they are not submitted and do so out of their own will, it could cause serious harm to those under their influence. The Apostles have a great responsibility, and that great responsibility is accompanied by a massive weight. They must ensure that they wholly die to themselves. They must ensure that they are led by His

Spirit and directed according to His will.

Some have the misunderstanding that the only Apostles were the original twelve appointed by Jesus. A thorough examination of Scripture refutes such an argument.

One, we have already examined how nowhere in Scripture does it say that any office will cease before another. But rather, Paul states that the Five-Fold Ministry as a whole will remain in operation until His return.

Two, to those who say that it was only those whom Jesus appointed Himself that were the Apostles, examining Ephesians 4:11 demonstrates that it is still Jesus who appoints the Apostles. Paul states, "He gave." "He" is in reference to Jesus.

Three, even in Scripture we see Apostles mentioned outside of the original twelve. For example Matthias (see Acts 1:12-26), Paul (see I Timothy 11:1 which was quoted earlier), Silas, and Timothy are mentioned together by Paul (see I Thessalonians 1:1, 2:6-7), Barnabas (see Acts 8:14), as well as others that are not directly mentioned as Apostles but based off of the wording of Scripture it seems to indicate that they were, such as Apollos (see I Corinthians 4:6-9).

It is seen, then, that the office of the Apostle was in operation outside of the original twelve. If it continued beyond them, and nowhere does it mention a sort of premature ending, then we should operate in the understanding that it is still present today.

Before continuing to the office of the Prophet, we must conclude by examining the ministry of an Apostle in action. Paul gave us great insight into what that exactly looks like: "The signs of a true apostle were performed among you with utmost patience, with signs and wonders and mighty works" (II Corinthians 12:12).

Paul begins his statement on recognizing true Apostleship by saying there will be particular "signs." This word in Greek is "sēmeion," and there are various ways one could translate it, but to borrow the verbiage of Jesus

Kingdom Progression

Himself, we could define it as the "fruit." The fruit of one who is truly an Apostle will be two things (condensing the final three listed by Paul into one group), that is "utmost patience" and "the miraculous."

It is interesting that Paul first lists the fruit of "utmost patience." I particularly find it interesting that Paul did not merely say that patience was a fruit of true Apostleship, but "utmost patience." The Greek word used here is "pas," referring simply to the totality of a thing. Therefore, perhaps one way we could phrase this would be, "complete patience." We could all readily define patience. It is an idea that is not foreign to us. Whether it is a practice not foreign to us could be debated, but that is not our focus here. Rather than define and dissect what patience is, I want to bring attention to how patience is cultivated.

Paul said in Romans 5:3, "Not only that, but we rejoice in our sufferings, knowing that suffering produces endurance." Further, James said in James 1:2-3, "Count it all joy, my brothers, when you meet trials of various kinds, for you know that the testing of your faith produces steadfastness." The word for "endurance" in Romans 5:3 and "steadfastness" in James 1:3 is the same Greek word, "hypomonē," which means "patience."

The fact that Apostles bear the fruit of complete patience indicates that they have borne great sufferings and trials. The great sufferings and trials that Apostles endure prepare them to minister to others with complete patience, truly displaying the heart of Jesus to that person in need. The Apostles Peter and John were unintentionally praised by the Council, not because they were so smart and knowledgeable: actually, they perceived them to be uneducated. But they saw in them something they had seen before, the character of Christ (see Acts 4:13).

Suffering and trials endured by the individual will either make them bitter or make them sweet. What determines the outcome of said sufferings and trials is the response of the individual in the midst of them. Who, or what, do you run to amid pain? One saying my Pastor has is, "Private Pain Processed Properly Produces Power."

Secondly, Paul states that the miraculous will be the fruit of an Apostle's ministry. Much could be said about this, but we will keep it plain. God uses the miraculous to confirm His Word. We stated earlier how the ministry of the Apostle is that of going. They are the first to step into new territories. They break open new possibilities to reach people, cultural groups, and nations. They deal a lot with "tilling the ground" (so to speak) of the hearts of those who have never heard the Gospel. God, then, will use the miraculous through the ministry of the Apostle to confirm what has been spoken. It is almost like a confirmation to those who are hearing these words for the first time. It helps them to trust and have faith, not in the one operating in the office, but in the Word of Truth they speak. That, then, opens the door for the seed to be planted in the ground that has been tilled.

The Prophet: Guides

"And he gave...the prophets" (Ephesians 4:11).

Keeping in line with how we examined the office of the Apostle, we will begin here by examining the position of the Prophet on the hand model. The Prophet is positioned on the index or pointer finger. This is fitting, for the pointer finger is used, more so than any other finger, to give direction. If someone asks you where something is, your automatic reaction is to point with your index finger and then say, "Over there," or something along those lines. This is exactly what the Office of the Prophet does: gives direction. Or, as the simplified definition states, to guide.

Something important to bring to attention is that many are confused about the difference between the office of the Prophet and the Gift of Prophecy. Many think that if one is ever used in the area of prophecy, they are therefore a

Kingdom Progression

Prophet. Such is not the case, though. We will examine what exactly the office of the Prophet is and how it functions, but first I want to bring to remembrance what was said about the Gifts of the Spirit in general. We examined I Corinthians 12:31 where Paul admonishes us to pursue the "higher gifts" which we translated as the Gift of the Spirit that was needed at that moment in time to meet that specific need. With the Gift of Prophecy, then, it is the individual allowing God to use them in a specific moment to speak His express Word for that moment. It does not necessarily mean they are called by God to guide, as the Prophet does, but to give specific guidance at the moment.

The office of the Prophet often works hand-in-hand with the Apostle. Paul stated, "and God has appointed in the church first apostles, second prophets..." (I Corinthians 12:28). Paul is conveying to us two specific things: one, the Apostle is the leader of the Five-Fold Ministry. They govern, they stand at the helm, and they are first. All of this aligns with what we spoke regarding the office of the Apostle. Two, the Prophet comes along right behind them. What exactly does the Prophet do? What does it mean to operate in the office of the Prophet?

The Greek word for "prophets" from Ephesians 4:11 is "prophētēs." This word means, defined vaguely, "a spokesman for another; a spokesman or interpreter for a deity." Given a more specific definition it means "one who, moved by the Spirit of God and hence his organ or spokesman, solemnly declares to men what he has received by inspiration, especially concerning future events, and in particular such as relate to the cause and kingdom of God and to human salvation."

"Spokesman" simply means "one who speaks for another." "Organ" means "the instrument or means of conveyance or communication." Furthermore, "interpreter" means "one that explains or expounds." Knowing these definitions, we see where we arrive at the definition of the

Prophet: to guide. One way in which Webster's Dictionary defines "guide" is "to lead or direct in a way; to conduct in a course or path; as, to guide an enemy or a traveler, who is not acquainted with the road or course."

Knowing such about what it means to be a Prophet, it is evident why Paul declared that the Prophet came along right behind the Apostle. For their ministries are strongly intertwined and often overlap. The Apostle, as discussed, is God's chosen leader for His Church and the Five-Fold Ministry. They stand at the helm and steer the ship. This requires great sensitivity to the will of God. The Prophet, then, works in sync with the Apostle to aid in the proper guidance of the Church. The Prophet will often expound upon the will of God that is being revealed to the Apostle so that it can be understood in a greater way.

A prominent example of this is found in the Book of Acts.

> While we were staying for many days, a prophet named Agabus came down from Judea. And coming to us, he took Paul's belt and bound his own feet and hands and said, "Thus says the Holy Spirit, 'This is how the Jews at Jerusalem will bind the man who owns this belt and deliver him into the hands of the Gentiles.'" When we heard this, we and the people there urged him not to go up to Jerusalem. Then Paul answered, "What are you doing, weeping and breaking my heart? For I am ready not only to be imprisoned but even to die in Jerusalem for the name of the Lord Jesus." And since he would not be persuaded, we ceased and said, "Let the will of the Lord be done."
> -Acts 21:10-14

Kingdom Progression

Here is what is seen: Paul knew the will of God for him was to go to Jerusalem. We aren't told exactly how Paul had discerned this, for the Book of Acts is not an exhaustive account of every event throughout the Book of Acts. Likely, God revealed this to him during a time of personal prayer. Paul had direction. Then God sent His Prophet, Agabus, to unveil a greater understanding as to what was to transpire in Jerusalem.

Another example of the relationship between the offices of the Prophet and the Apostle is seen in an earlier account involving the same Prophet, Agabus.

> Now in these days prophets came down from Jerusalem to Antioch. And one of them named Agabus stood up and foretold by the Spirit that there would be a great famine over all the world (this took place in the days of Claudius). So the disciples determined, every one according to his ability, to send relief to the brothers living in Judea. And they did so, sending it to the elders by the hand of Barnabas and Saul.
> -Acts 11:27-30

The Prophet Agabus came to the Church at Antioch, where many of the leaders of the Church (the Apostles) were stationed. The Prophet revealed what was to come in regards to the famine, so the Apostles, then, riding on the guidance of the Prophet, led and directed the Church appropriately to meet the need that was to come.

The distinction between the Gift of Prophecy and the office of the Prophet is clear. God uses the Gift of Prophecy to give specific direction for a moment, for a situation. However, God uses the Prophet to guide His Church and aid the Apostle in the leading of the Church. We are told in Amos 3:7, "For the Lord GOD does nothing without revealing his secret to his servants the prophets." All that God desires to do, He will reveal plainly to the Prophets. The Prophets will then clearly speak the will and direction of God. This is the role of the office of the Prophet: to guide.

The Evangelist: Gathers

"And he gave…the evangelist" (Ephesians 4:11).

The Office of the Evangelist is represented by the third or center finger. If you rest all your fingers up against one another while stretching them out, you will see that the third finger extends out the furthest. This represents the role of the Evangelist, for they reach out further than any office of ministry. This is not to say that the Evangelist does more than any other office, for they all work in unity together, each doing their part. However, the role of the Evangelist extends the furthest beyond the metaphoric and literal walls of the Church. Every office operates both within and outside of the Church, but the Office of the Evangelist spends the majority of its time outside the Church, more so than any other office.

The Greek word here is "euangelistēs," which is translated as "an evangelist," or "a bringer of glad tidings" which is in reference to the Gospel. We addressed a common misunderstanding that exists between the Gift of Prophecy and the Office of the Prophet. There exists a misunderstanding with the Office of the Evangelist as well. Many misunderstand the offices of the Five-Fold Ministry as things that all mature Christians are to partake of. However, when one examines Paul's wording, he refers to these five ministries as specific offices, not just works of the mature Christian. All are called to be a light by allowing His Light to shine forth from us and to make disciples (which we will discuss in the final chapter). Many refer to engaging in such as "evangelism." Thus, the misunderstanding is that by "evangelizing" we are operating as Evangelists. Again, there

Kingdom Progression

is a distinction between obeying the Great Commission (see Matthew 28:19) and operating in the Office of the Evangelist.

When examining the Office of the Apostle, we noted how it says that Philip, who was identified as an Evangelist (see Acts 21:8), "proclaimed to them the Christ" (Acts 8:5). Thus, we surmised that this rightly identified the role of the Evangelist. If we examine the ministry of Philip, since he was specifically identified as an Evangelist, we see that he was constantly reaching out, constantly on the move, and constantly seeking after another. We aren't told much about his ministry, but this is what we do see: one, he went to Samaria and proclaimed the Gospel to them (see Acts 8:4-8); two, he then went to a road that connects Jerusalem to Gaza to preach to an Ethiopian Eunuch (see Acts 8:26-38); and finally, the Spirit then took him miraculously to Azotus. From there he went to Caesarea and preached to them (see Acts 8:39-40). It is as I pointed out at the start, the Evangelist's primary focus is outside the Church. This is clearly displayed in the ministry of Philip, for he was constantly going. Going where? To the next town, city, and country that needed to hear the Gospel.

This is why the Evangelist has been given the summarized role, "to gather." There are several good definitions given by the Webster's Dictionary for the word "gather:" "to bring together; to collect a number of separate things into one place or into one aggregate body; to get in harvest; to reap or cut and bring into barns or stores; to assemble; to congregate; to bring persons into one place; to collect in abundance; to accumulate; to amass." There are others, but these adequately convey the point. Again, yes, all are called to shine His Light and to make disciples. The call to do such cannot be left solely to the Evangelists. However, the Office of the Evangelist operates at a much higher level of such. You may make a disciple here and there. You might see a couple of people come into the Church through you operating in discipleship. Comparatively, the Evangelist will gather in hundreds, thousands, and let's speak in faith and say even millions. Without the Office of the Evangelist in full operation, the Church will not grow as God desires. For it is the Evangelists who are always out, always reaching, always gathering, always calling, always going. Those who are not Evangelists do these things in part, but for the Evangelists, this is who they are.

Evangelists are the people that everyone wants to be friends with. Everyone is simply drawn to them and no one knows exactly why. Is it their charm? Or charisma? Their easy-going demeanor? Something else? All of the above? What is often said of them is, "Oh, they have a great personality!" This may be true, and I am not downplaying that they might indeed have a great personality. More accurately though, the true reason why all are so drawn to them is due to the gift of God on their life, the Office in which He has called them. God would not send out one to be His Evangelist, to gather, if they were pessimistic, dreary, monotone, and so on. Such a person would drive others away, not pull them in. God has gifted these individuals with the divine gift of genuine hospitality. The Webster's Dictionary defines "hospitality" as "the act or practice of receiving and entertaining strangers or guests without reward, or with kind and generous liberality." Meaning, an Evangelist never meets a stranger, only a new friend who they welcome as family. This is what draws people unto them and allows the Evangelist to gather in abundance and bring such into the Church.

The Pastor: Guards

"And he gave...the shepherds" (Ephesians 4:11).

The Office of the Pastor (Shepherd) is represented by the ring finger. This is very interesting, for the ring finger represents commitment or relationship. Something very interesting is seen when one examines Webster's Dictionary

Kingdom Progression

definition of "commitment:" it conveys that this word refers to putting one into prison. In essence, this word conveys one who is locked in, bound, tied down, and so on. Furthermore, "relationship" (according to Webster's Dictionary) is a useless word, and it prefers "affinity," which it defines as "agreement; relation; conformity; resemblance; connection."

What is seen by these definitions is that the Office of the Pastor is one of intimacy. The Pastor has a deep connection to the particular body of believers they reside over. I have seen Pastors who have operated in their role at a distance from the Body. They close themselves off and shut themselves behind closed doors. They don't engage in close friendships with those in the Church. However, the Pastor is meant to dwell among the people. The Pastor is meant to be a part of the Body that he has been positioned over. Looking back to the definitions of "affinity," the Pastor is meant to be in agreement with the people, relate with them, be conformed (in unity) with them, resemble them, and connect to them. None of these things can be achieved from a distance but only from a place of intimacy. Only from a place of genuine knowing.

The word used for the Office of the Pastor is "poimēn" which means "a shepherd." Another definition of this word is "he to whose care and control others have committed themselves, and whose precepts they follow."

The Office of the Pastor is a very unique one. It has become the most common in our day and age, for we label every ministry some sort of "pastor." In actuality, the true Office of a Pastor is very unique. One could say that those who operate in this office most evidently reflect the heart of God. For Jesus declared, "I am the good shepherd. The good shepherd lays down his life for the sheep. He who is a hired hand and not a shepherd, who does not own the sheep, sees the wolf coming and leaves the sheep and flees, and the wolf snatches them and scatters them. He flees because he is a hired hand and cares nothing for the sheep. I am the good shepherd. I know my own and my own know me." (John 10:11-14). The word "shepherd" here from this passage is the same as from Ephesians 4:11. "Good" is "kalos," which means "beautiful, handsome, excellent, eminent, choice, surpassing, precious, useful, suitable, commendable, admirable." Meaning, Jesus is the Shepherd above all others. He is the "excellent Shepherd," the "surpassing Shepherd." Within this passage, Jesus conveys to us the true role of a Shepherd: they lay down their life for the sheep, and they know the sheep and are known by the sheep.

Those who are called into this office bear a heavy weight, not just because they watch over the Church (the flock), but it is as I said, they reflect the very heart of God. Those in the Office of the Pastor are the most seen out of all the offices. They are the most recognized. Oftentimes, how individuals view God is based on their experience with their Pastor.

We are given several good examples of what a shepherd does and how they tend the flock they reside over. Looking first at the life of David, we read this in I Samuel 17, "But David said to Saul, 'Your servant used to keep sheep for his father. And when there came a lion, or a bear, and took a lamb from the flock, I went after him and struck him and delivered it out of his mouth. And if he arose against me, I caught him by his beard and struck him and killed him'" (v.34-35). Jesus told us this: "What man of you, having a hundred sheep, if he has lost one of them, does not leave the ninety-nine in the open country, and go after the one that is lost, until he finds it? And when he has found it, he lays it on his shoulders, rejoicing" (Luke 15:4-5).

Here is what is seen from these passages (combining the two passages into one flow of thought): the Shepherd is concerned about the whole flock (the Church), not just the flock as a whole, but each sheep or lamb that makes up the flock. If the Shepherd has a flock of a hundred but loses one, they do not shrug their shoulders and say, "At least I

Kingdom Progression

still have ninety-nine." Rather, they will switch their focus temporarily off of the whole and onto the one. It does not matter if the one was snared by the enemy or wandered off. Either way, the Shepherd intently seeks after them and willingly fights off the enemy that desires to consume them. If the one is not snared away, but wanders, when they are found, the Shepherd does not scold them or punish them. Rather, the Shepherd will put the sheep onto his shoulders (bearing their burdens [see Galatians 6:2]) and rejoice that they are found and returning to the flock.

Another crucial aspect of the Pastor that bears examination comes from one of the final one-on-one interactions between Jesus and Peter.

> When they had finished breakfast, Jesus said to Simon Peter, "Simon, son of John, do you love me more than these?" He said to him, "Yes, Lord; you know that I love you." He said to him, "Feed my lambs." He said to him a second time, "Simon, son of John, do you love me?" He said to him, "Yes, Lord; you know that I love you." He said to him, "Tend my sheep." He said to him the third time, "Simon, son of John, do you love me?" Peter was grieved because he said to him the third time, "Do you love me?" and he said to him, "Lord, you know everything; you know that I love you." Jesus said to him, "Feed my sheep."
> -John 21:15-17

One thing is immediately seen: the Shepherd's ability to care for the Church stems from the level of love for Him in which they abide. This points back to what I said earlier: the role of the Pastor most clearly reflects the heart of God.

We see Jesus give three commands to Peter (which

he operated first as an Apostle and then as a Pastor): one, "Feed my lambs." Two, "Tend my sheep." And three, "Feed my sheep."

First, "Feed my lambs." "Feed" here is "boskō," and it refers to making readily available what is necessary for nourishment and growth. In regard to sheep, this refers to providing them with open plains and pastures in which they can graze. In regard to the Church, this refers to providing them with the truth of God that is needed for them to grow and develop in Him. "Lamb" is "arnion" which refers to an infant, or little lamb. One that is immature. One that is not developed. Therefore, the first command that Jesus gave Peter as a Shepherd was to provide the necessary nourishment that those who are infants in the Church need to grow and develop. Referring to one as an infant is not an insult, it simply points to one who has been Born Again only recently and needs to be nourished, just as a literal infant would.

Two, "Tend my sheep." "Tend" is "poimainō" which can also be translated as "to feed." But this word is more of a vague word, encompassing all the roles of a shepherd over a flock of sheep. It can refer to feeding them, keeping watch over them, or protecting them. "Sheep" is "probaton" which refers to a fully grown, fully developed sheep. What Jesus is conveying, then, is that as the individual grows and matures and is no longer an infant, it does not negate the need for a Shepherd in their life. Even when mature, the sheep still need one to tend to them. A Christian will always need a Shepherd to properly tend to them, lest they come under attack and have no one to fight for them and to ensure that what they are eating is truly good for them (distinguishing between the doctrine and false doctrine).

Finally, "Feed my sheep." The Greek words for "feed" and "sheep" are two we have already examined, "boskō" and "probaton." Jesus here is specifically pointing to the truth that even when one is mature and grown, they still

Kingdom Progression

need a Shepherd to feed them and give them the necessary nutrients. There is no such thing as a Christian who is so mature that they no longer need the Body and their Pastor. We've demonstrated these truths when examining private and corporate devotion in chapter two and when talking about the necessity of the Body in unity when speaking on the spiritual Gifts.

Through all of this, we can see why the definitive role of "to guard" was attributed to the Pastor. Webster's Dictionary defines "guard" as "to secure against injury, loss or attack; to protect; to defend; to keep in safety." All of this falls perfectly in line with all that we have discussed here regarding the Office of the Pastor (Shepherd).

The Teacher: Grounds

"And he gave…teachers" (Ephesians 4:11).

The final office within the Five-Fold Ministry that we come to is that of the Teacher. Starting once again by examining the hand model that simplifies the roles of the differing offices, we see that the Teacher is represented by the pinky finger. This may seem insignificant, for what does the pinky do? How does it compare to the rest of the fingers? It is exceedingly easy to overlook the pinky when compared to the other fingers: this is often how it also is with the Office of the Teacher when compared to the other offices. What many don't realize is that the pinky does play a crucial role on the hand; the pinky finger provides balance. This is an accurate demonstration of the role of the Teacher: providing balance.

Webster's Dictionary provides several good and helpful definitions of "balance," all of which reflect the same idea. The underlying idea behind balance is such: to determine the equality or the difference between different things. This can be both literal and figurative. It can refer to balancing out two objects to see if they are the same, or if they are different, and how they are different. Or it can refer to mental assessment, making mental judgments between two opposing ideas, and finding the balance between the two. This understanding beautifully encompasses the role of the Teacher.

The Teacher is the most hands-on of all the offices. As we discussed previously, they operate on an individual level. The Teachers are the most in-tune with what the Body is being fed, for they actively judge what is being fed to the Body to determine its true nature. This takes us back to the idea of balance, comparing two separate objects to determine their equality or difference; in balancing, you must always have a reference, the thing which holds the standard. This is the thing in which all others are compared to or weighed against. You then bring in an outside object to judge it against the standard. This is what the Teacher does. The standard they have to compare and weigh everything against is the Word of God. The Teacher knows the Word in a greater manner compared to all the other offices, for that is directly what they deal with. Having the standard, the Word of God, the Teacher then takes the ideas and philosophies of men and compares them to the standard. Do they balance out? Or is there a difference in weight?

One way in which the role of the Teacher could be defined would be to filter. A filter's entire job is to distinguish. Take, for example, a coffee filter. When making coffee, coffee grounds are first placed into the filter. Then, hot water is poured over the grounds to pass through the grounds with the result of brewing coffee. When a filter works properly, there will be no coffee grounds in the coffee liquid. However, if the filter is faulty, punctured, or any such thing, one will find grounds in the coffee, thus creating a gritty and bitter aftertaste. The Office of the Teacher works the same: they are expressly used by God to filter out the junk of man's ideas that don't align with His Word. When the Teacher is operating properly, the end result will be a pure, untainted product. However, if the Office of the Teacher is not being enacted properly, there could be a lot of unwanted "grounds" that enter the Body.

Understanding all of this is why the Office of the Teacher was given the simplified definition: to ground. In this context, Webster's Dictionary defines "ground" as: "foundation, that which supports any thing; fundamental cause, primary reason or original principle; first principles, as the grounds of religion." By acting as one who balances and filters by the Word of God, the Teacher thereby grounds the Body with the foundation of doctrine and provides insight into the fundamental principles of doctrine.

I mentioned when discussing the Office of the Pastor how they, more so than any other, display and convey the very heart of God and are the most intimate. Here, when discussing the Teacher, I mentioned how they are the most hands-on and personal. Is this a contradiction? No. For the Pastor knows the Body in a greater way than any other office, but the Teacher knows the Word that is presented to the Body in a greater way than any other office.

"Teacher" from Ephesians 4:11 is "didaskalos," and along with "teacher," this word can also mean "master," or "doctor." Meaning, this does not simply refer to one who teaches, but it also refers to one who operates at a distinguished level of understanding in reference to a particular area. This is obvious by the definitions of "master" and "doctor." For "doctor" is a distinguished title reserved only for those who dwell at a superior level of knowledge in a particular field. Furthermore, "master" refers to one who rules over, or is head over. Having this understanding of the Teacher, we can then better understand a teaching of Paul's that we looked at earlier in part. "And God has appointed in the church first apostles, second prophets, third teachers..." (I Corinthians 12:28). Even though the Teacher is often overlooked, according to Paul, it is third in line regarding authority in the Church. It is easy to understand why such is the case after examining all that we have here. The Teacher is the final authority on what is fed to the Church.

Throughout this book, we have, at several points, mentioned how being "able to teach" is not the same as operating in the Office of the Teacher, even though many think such is the case. After examining all that we have here, it is exceedingly evident that they are not the same thing. Yes, Teachers are "able to teach," obviously, just as any office or ministry or mature Christian ought to be "able to teach." The difference is, as previously mentioned, the Teachers are the final authority on what is fed to the flock. They distinguish between truth and falsehood by weighing all against the Word of God.

The Teacher must be in operation within the Church so that false doctrine be kept at bay. If we forsake allowing the Teacher to be fully present, we run the risk of allowing the Body to become tainted with the gritty bitterness of the "grounds" that passed through the faulty filter.

Operating in the Five-Fold Ministry

When discussing the spiritual Gifts in the previous chapter, we ended by examining how we are to operate in such, that is, love. We then, using Paul's breakdown of love, properly defined what exactly love is and what it looks like. Here, at the close of this chapter, we will end our discussion of the Five-Fold Ministry in like fashion.

Paul, after discussing the purpose and duration of the offices, then states, "rather, speaking the truth in love..." (Ephesians 4:15). This, then, is how we are to operate within the different offices.

"Speaking the truth" is one word in Greek: "alētheuō." "Alētheuō" means "to speak or maintain the truth; to act truly or sincerely." In other words, this word points to not just being well-versed in the verbiage and mental understanding of what is true but also personally living it out. In essence, this word encompasses the well-known phrase, "Practice what you preach." The ones who operate in the different offices are to be examples of the one true doctrine in both word and deed, speaking and living the truth.

How we are to act in "speaking the truth" is "love." "Love" here is "agapē" which expressly refers to the love of God. As we operate in the office to which we are called, we must do so in love. Moreover, not just any idea or definition of love, but we must operate in His love (which we thoroughly defined previously). To repeat for the sake of clarity, His love is patient, and kind, does not envy or boast, is not arrogant or rude, does not insist on its own way, is not irritable or resentful, and does not rejoice in wrongdoing, but rather in truth. His love bears, believes, hopes, and endures for eternity.

We can have all the technical understanding of the Five-Fold Ministry in the world, but if we do not "speak the truth in love," it is all for nothing. If we do not operate in accordance with His character and nature, then we act in and of ourselves. As long as we act in and of ourselves, we work contrary to His will and against His Kingdom. As Jesus stated, "Whoever is not with me is against me, and whoever does not gather with me scatters" (Matthew 12:30). We need to actively ensure that we are in proper alignment with Him and His standard. For every office, every gift, and every ministry is of Him and under Him. Thereby, to properly operate in such, we must be as well.

Conclusion

The Five-Fold Ministry is essential to the Church and the proper growth and development thereof. We must allow it to operate in the manner which God desires. As stated previously, every kingdom has a king, and every king establishes those to help him rule and govern the people. God is our King, and we are of His Kingdom, the people of

His Name. The Five-Fold Ministry is the government of God enacted to aid Him in leading His people. Without such in operation, God cannot lead His people in the manner which He desires.

Moreover, it is not simply that the offices need to be in operation, but they need to be operated in properly. Again, this is in love: His love. Even if we do not fully understand the total nature of the office He has called us to, as long as we operate in what we do know according to His character and nature, He will reveal to us more perfectly how He desires for us to operate.

6
The Call to All

Throughout this book, we have examined a plethora of topics, from the Kingdom of God, to how God judges one trustworthy or not, to what it means to operate in ministry and what the anointing is, to understanding the spiritual Gifts of God and the Five-Fold Ministry. All that we have so far discussed converges on this final topic, which is why I have positioned it here at the end. For all that we do in and for His Kingdom, every ministry we operate in, every role we fill, every Spiritual Gift we operate in, and every Five-Fold Ministry Office we are called to, is all driven by one, singular purpose: "Go therefore and make disciples..." (Matthew 28:19).

It does not matter where you are called to. Maybe all you feel called to do in the Church is clean the restrooms. Great, that is a legitimate need of the Church. Even still, the foundation of that call to clean the restrooms is to go make disciples. Or maybe you feel called to one of the Five-Fold Ministry Offices, leading the Church. That's great too, for God's order of government needs to be in operation. However, while abiding in those offices, we cannot forsake that the fundamental call is to go and make disciples.

If ever we lose sight of this commission (The Great Commission as it has been dubbed), then we have lost sight of the true purpose for every ministry, every gift, and every office. If ever we lose sight of making disciples, then we have forsaken the mission of furthering His Kingdom and have begun to build our own. We cannot view ministry and operating in the Gifts of the Spirit and abiding in the Five-Fold Ministry as a "cushy" job where we get to just sit back and dictate to all the "inferior" people under us. This sounds ridiculous, but it is more of a prevalent mindset than one might realize. In all that we do for God and His Kingdom, if we truly desire to operate for and in such, it must be done with the motive of making disciples.

What I aim to do here at the close, then, is to walk through what one might define as "how to teach." I do not mean that this is going to be a lesson on the proper manner in which one should teach a class. Rather, we are going to look at essentials that need to be understood and operated in when attempting to make a disciple. After this, we are going to look at "whom to teach." By this I do not mean that we only teach certain individuals or are judgmental or any such thing, for the Bible says that God shows no partiality, as we have mentioned (see Acts 10:24-25; Romans 2:1; and James 2:1), so we ought to also show no partiality. What I mean by "whom to teach" is that we are going to look at and properly define what it means to be a disciple. For if we are ever going to make disciples, we must first understand what it means to be one.

Know Them

If you examine the Book of Acts, you will find several different instances wherein an Apostle (particularly Peter or Paul) was speaking to individuals or a group of individuals. It is interesting when you carefully read how they spoke to the different groups that they spoke to.

In Acts 2 we witness the birth of the Church after the outpouring of His Spirit. Many were roundabout that heard this supernatural occurrence and were confused by it. Starting in verse 14 and going through verse 40 we read Peter's response to them, the first sermon of the Apostolic Church. In it we see Peter quote a few Old Testament Scriptures, Joel 2:28-32 and Psalms 16:8-11, and then use those Scriptures to explain and convey what exactly they had all just witnessed. To whom did Peter speak? The Book of Acts identified them as "men of Israel…" (Acts 2:22) and not just native

Kingdom Progression

Israelites, but they were "devout" (Acts 2:5). What we see, then, is that Peter knew his audience. They were individuals who knew the Scriptures for themselves and knew it well since they were defined as "devout." He knew that for them to understand and believe, he had to speak to them at their level. Therefore, he opened up the Scriptures and used them to speak to them. If he had not used what they knew, they would not have believed.

Jumping forward, we read in Acts 10 of the Gospel first being preached to the Gentiles. Here again, we see that it is Peter speaking to these individuals. We examined previously how he spoke to his fellow Jewish brothers and sisters. Did he speak to these Gentiles in the same manner? No. The level of understanding the Gentiles had was not the same as the Jews, for they were not birthed in that same culture and surrounded by the Old Testament texts all their lives. What then did Peter speak to them? Starting in verse 34 and going to verse 43, what we see Peter preach to these Gentile men and women was simply Jesus. Peter preached to them Jesus: what He came to do, what He did do, and what all that did for them. Peter concluded his sermon with this: "And he commanded us to preach to the people and to testify that he is the one appointed by God to be judge of the living and the dead. To him all the prophets bear witness that everyone who believes in him receives forgiveness of sins through his name" (Acts 10:42-43).

With one last example, let's look this time at the Apostle Paul. In Acts 17 we read of Paul arriving in Athens. His original plan after arriving was to await the arrival of Silas and Timothy but was overwhelmed by the pressing need of Athens. What was this pressing need? The city was consumed in idolatry. Meaning, these were not people who knew anything about the One true God or His Word. If Paul went to these people and preached to them from the Scriptures, it would have gone right over their heads. Rather, he spoke to them on their level of understanding. We read, starting in verse 22 and going through verse 31, Paul's sermon to these people. What he taught these people were very foundational things because they were so consumed by all of their various idols. He had to explain who God was, the proper way in which to worship Him, how He is not far from us but very near and easy to seek after, and the need to repent. These were very foundational teachings, but this was what they needed to hear, for they could not have received anything more complex

The first thing we need to understand, then, is who we are talking to. Where are they in life? What is their level of understanding? Are they self-proclaimed atheists? Pantheists? Polytheists? If they do believe in God, how much do they know? Do they know anything about the Bible? Or do they simply acknowledge the idea that God probably exists (their wording)? Before you can teach anyone anything, you must first make it personal and know them. This means that, at first, there may not be a whole lot of biblical talk, but rather just getting to know them: talking to them about their life, their family, their hobbies, whatever. The goal of these conversations is not simply small talk. Rather, it is to judge where they are. You have to make a conscious effort to point every conversation back to God, because based off how they talk about God is how you will determine where they are.

Know it for Yourself

Before you can truly talk to anyone about God or His Word, you first need to know it for yourself. For you to know it for yourself, you must've at first sought it out for yourself. We cannot operate in the mindset that God's anointing will work in us, and He will speak through us the answer that we didn't know. There may be times where He does this in the life of an individual who has intentionally sought Him and His truth but had not fully realized that certain, particular truth. However, we cannot allow this mindset to be our crutch. When speaking on the Holy Spirit working in us, Jesus said that the Holy Spirit would "bring to your remembrance all that I have said to you" (John 14:26). How can He bring to remembrance something that is not first there? We must get into the Word and study it for ourselves. Also, we cannot study simply to have good sermon notes. We must study to know the truth for ourselves. If we study simply to have good sermon notes, we study for man and not for the truth of God, because we seek to sound good, not to be right.

Looking to the words of the Apostle Paul, "Paul, an apostle—not from men nor through man, but through Jesus Christ and God the Father, who raised him from the dead—and all the brothers who are with me, to the churches of Galatia...For am I now seeking the approval of man, or of God? Or am I trying to please man? If I were still trying to please man, I would not be a servant of Christ. For I would have you know, brothers, that the gospel that was preached by me is not man's gospel. For I did not receive it from any man, nor was I taught it, but I received it through a revelation of Jesus Christ" (Galatians 1:1-2, 10-12). Paul did not seek revelation to gain favor and standing among the Churches. Rather, he sought greater revelation so that he might know Him in a greater way.

Returning to the idea that we have to know it for ourselves before we can share it with others, in Deuteronomy 6:4-5 we read what has become known as "The Shema." The Shema was and is central in the life of a devout Jew. Every morning they would wake up and speak it, likewise, every night before going to bed. Not just that, though, for this would also be uttered over the newborns among the Jews, so that it was the first thing they heard. This would also be uttered over one who was about to die, so it would be the last thing they heard. Our focus is on the verses that follow this integral command. Immediately after giving this to the people, God spoke and said, "And these words that I command you today shall be on your heart. You shall teach them diligently to your children, and shall talk of them when you sit in your house, and when you walk by the way, and when you lie down, and when you rise. You shall bind them as a sign on your hand, and they shall be as frontlets between your eyes. You shall write them on the doorposts of your house and on your gates" (Deuteronomy 6:6-9).

Here is what we see from this passage. First, the Word of God is to be stored in the heart of the individual. This implies a sincere and intense seeking after the Word. Verse 6 states that the Word is to be "on" the heart. This word "on" is very powerful: it is "'al." "Al" refers to the yoke that was placed around the neck of the oxen. The power of this is understood when you understand the purpose of the yoke. The yoke was positioned to, one, keep the oxen in line: it kept them from wandering astray. Two, it gave control of the oxen to the one working the field. What we see, then, is that when the Word of the Lord is truly bound up in our hearts (after we have intensely sought after it) it becomes the yoke that keeps us properly aligned with where God wants us and gives Him complete control to guide us where He wants us to go.

Only after we have truly stored up His Word by intensely seeking after it and allowing it to grab hold of us do we see the command to "go and teach." One thing my Pastor says is, "You cannot lead others to an experience you have not had." This truth is affirmed throughout Scripture and is so here as well. For if we try to teach our children (which could refer to literal or spiritual children, as the Apostle Paul considered himself the spiritual father of individuals like Timothy) before we know it for ourselves, what are we teaching them? Also, if we try and talk about it before we know it, what are we talking about? Odds are we will end up teaching and talking about false doctrine that is easier for our carnality to cope with than the true Word of God that convicts and transforms.

Kingdom Progression

The verses that follow the command to teach our children and talk about it to them are also very significant. After we teach it and talk about it, we are not then allowed to loosen our grip on it, let go of it, lose sight of it, or any such thing. Rather, the call to greater awareness of His Word is given after we teach and talk about it. As it says, we are to "bind them as a sign on your hand, and they shall be as frontlets between your eyes. You shall write them on the doorposts of your house and on your gates" (Deuteronomy 6:8-9). In other words, His Word is to always go before us in all that we do. It is to always be on our minds and given our attention.

We have already talked about the importance of knowing His Word in the chapter, Can God Trust You? Therefore, I will not do so here again. However, we cannot forsake the integral step of truly knowing the Word of God for ourselves before we make disciples.

Walking in Faith, Not Insecurity

A common excuse that people often use in an attempt to avoid having to speak to people is that they are not good at talking to people. Maybe they have a stutter or a lisp, or maybe they're simply shy, whatever the case may be. Often, in such cases, people will look to Moses as their scapegoat, stating how God gave Aaron to Moses because he was "slow of speech and of tongue" (Exodus 4:10), as the Bible words it. People who look to this example as their defense do not truly understand what transpired in this passage. Let's look at it to gain a proper understanding of it.

> But Moses said to the LORD, "Oh, my Lord, I am not eloquent, either in the past or since you have spoken to your servant, but I am slow of speech and of tongue." Then the LORD said to him, "Who has made man's mouth? Who

> makes him mute, or deaf, or seeing, or blind? Is it not I, the LORD? Now therefore go, and I will be with your mouth and teach you what you shall speak." But he said, "Oh, my Lord, please send someone else." Then the anger of the LORD was kindled against Moses and he said, "Is there not Aaron, your brother, the Levite? I know that he can speak well. Behold, he is coming out to meet you, and when he sees you, he will be glad in his heart. You shall speak to him and put the words in his mouth, and I will be with your mouth and with his mouth and will teach you both what to do.
> -Exodus 4:10-15

    Looking at the context of this passage, we see God appear to Moses in the burning bush that was not consumed and speak out of such. He calls to Moses, stating that He has seen the afflictions of His people and has heard their cries and is going to deliver them and desires to use Moses to do so. Moses is naturally shocked and asks the questions that we would all ask in his position. Then we see a shift transpire in Exodus 4: Moses becomes overwhelmed by doubt and fear. God responds by giving him three powerful signs that will utterly convey that he had been sent by YAHWEH (see Exodus 4:1-9). That is where we then find ourselves at the point of our quoted passage. Moses cannot deny the power of the signs and how effective they would be. Understanding such, he then flips the page away from the people's belief to his lack of ability. He states that, as mentioned previously, he is "slow of speech and of tongue." God counters this argument by saying, "Who has made man's mouth? Who makes him mute, or deaf, or seeing, or blind? Is it not I, the LORD? Now therefore go, and I will be with your mouth and teach you what you shall speak." He is conveying to Moses

Kingdom Progression

that it is not about his ability or lack thereof, but that He will be in control of his mouth and speak through him. We've examined how anointing transcends talent or natural ability. Moses, overcome with insecurity, doubt, fear, and lack of faith in God's ability to do what He said He would do, again questions the Almighty. We are told that this angered the LORD. This word "anger" is "'aph," and it refers to how the nostrils flare when one is passionately and intensely angry. God's anger toward Moses is understood even greater when the word "kindled" is examined. This is "charah," and it can mean a multitude of things all along the lines of hot, burning, heat, scorching, and so on. Specifically, in regards to anger, it means "the heat of anger." Therefore, God's anger burned so hotly against Moses because of his lack of faith that the Bible had to use the imagery of His nostrils flaring due to His anger against Moses.

It is only after this interaction that we see God appoint Aaron to be Moses' mouth, not before. What we see, then, is that appointing Aaron was not God's original plan. It was Moses' insecurity and lack of faith that drove God to deviate from His plan. God knew Moses' struggle with speaking, and that is exactly why He called him. Remember how we talked about how God chooses the things that don't make sense to accomplish certain tasks. He does this so that no one can receive the glory but Him. This is exactly what was transpiring here, but Moses refused to operate in faith and forced God to execute plan B.

Thus, we understand that using the example of Moses as our defense for walking in insecurity and not faith is not a very good defense after all. For the Lord was angry with Moses. Do you truly desire for God to kindle His anger against you? Or would you rather operate in faith and understand that it's not about you, and it never was? It has always been about Him and His work and His will. We just have to walk in faith, trusting that God will always make up for our lack.

Kristopher David Grepke

Humility

    We have already looked at humility when speaking on what it means to truly be a minister of God, so I will not reiterate all that has already been said. However, humility is a key aspect in the area of making disciples. For we must remember, one, it is God doing the work through you. It is not your natural ability. It is His grace on full display in you. If the words that exit your mouth bring understanding and revelation to another, remember, He put those words in you. Also, humility is crucial in the way in which events unfold. You may have a particular idea as to how a certain chain of events ought to go. You think that if you do this thing in this particular fashion, or word it just like this, or go to this certain spot, it'll all work out perfectly. Then, thirty seconds into it, God upheaves your plans and ideas. When this happens— not if but when—we must have humility. We have to understand that we don't see all and know all and understand all. We don't know exactly what the individual needs to see and hear for faith to be birthed and for them to walk in obedience. We might think we do, but we don't. We have to recognize that our way is not the best. Rather, His way is the only way.

    We've looked at it previously when talking about waiting amid the anointing process, but Psalms 147:5 and I John 3:20 convey how God knows all things and sees all things. His understanding is beyond our level of comprehension. Therefore, when He redirects your agenda, don't try and force it back. We've also talked about being in unity with God and submitting to His will. If we continually try and redirect His plan and do things our way, eventually, God will take His hands off us and let us drive ourselves into destruction. We must have humility when approaching discipleship and allow God to work through us and around us in the manner which He desires, because He knows best.

Kingdom Progression

Operating in Love

The key aspect of dwelling in true humility and making disciples is love. The Apostle Paul said it like this: "If I speak in the tongues of men and of angels, but have not love, I am a noisy gong or a clanging cymbal. And if I have prophetic powers, and understand all mysteries and all knowledge, and if I have all faith, so as to remove mountains, but have not love, I am nothing. If I give away all I have, and if I deliver up my body to be burned, but have not love, I gain nothing" (I Corinthians 13:1-3). We all know this passage well, some by heart. We have quoted it and heard it more times than we can likely count. Unfortunately, we often overlook what Paul is conveying to us here.

In our society, we very often dwell in a mindset and attitude of "give and get." We think, "Well, if I do this, then I'll get this." Or, "If this is what I give, then this will be my reward!" We do and give with the motive of receiving in return. This is not what it means to operate in love. We think, "Well, I am doing it for them, so it's love." In actuality, it's not for them, it's really for you. You've simply put on the face that it's for them. If our motivation is what we get in return, then what we did was never out of love but selfish gain. When operating out of such a place, all that we do is in vain. This is why the Bible says, "It is more blessed to give than to receive" (Acts 20:35). But not just to give, "… for God loves a cheerful giver" (II Corinthians 9:7). The attitude in which one gives conveys the level of love in which they operate. To truly operate out of love is to give with no intention of receiving in return. To love is to freely give (freely meaning there is no hidden cost).

John stated in his first epistle, "Beloved, let us love one another, for love is from God, and whoever loves has been born of God and knows God. Anyone who does not love does not know God, because God is love. In this the love of God was made manifest among us, that God sent his only Son into the world, so that we might live through him. In this is love, not that we have loved God but that he loved us and sent his Son to be the propitiation for our sins. Beloved, if God so loved us, we also ought to love one another. No one has ever seen God; if we love one another, God abides in us and his love is perfected in us" (I John 4:7-12).

Here is what we see: anyone who truly dwells in love, lives in Him, for He is love. If we do not operate in love, we do not live in Him but only in ourselves. The only way people see and experience God, outside of their personal experience, is through the love that exudes from us. Taking this back to what Paul declared about love: when you reach out to others and teach them but do not do so out of love, they are not seeing any aspect of God, they are only seeing you. For it is only when you dwell in and operate out of a state of love (but not just any love, His love) that people truly see Him in you. All that we do is in vain if it is not done in love. For what are the three things that Paul declares one truly is when love is not at the center of all that they do and say? He states that they, one, are loud and annoying; two, are nothing at all; and three, gain nothing (even though that was their entire motivation: to gain).

Another important passage on love is Matthew 22:35-39: "And one of them, a lawyer, asked him a question to test him. 'Teacher, which is the great commandment in the Law?' And he said to him, 'You shall love the Lord your God with all your heart and with all your soul and with all your mind. This is the great first commandment. And a second is like it: You shall love your neighbor as yourself.'"

Here is what we see: the first Great Commandment is that we are to love Him with everything that we are. This must come first. This takes us back to what we already examined, that you have to first know it for yourself. For it is only after you know Him and His love for yourself that you can then share Him and His love. Furthermore, He said, "and

Kingdom Progression

a second is like it," implying that the second is comparable to, or equal to, the first. Meaning, "to love your neighbor as yourself" is just as important as "love the Lord your God."

When speaking on love, Jesus said, "Greater love has no one than this, that someone lay down his life for his friends" (John 15:13). We know that He was referring to His sacrifice for our sins. This text can be applied to us too, however. For there is no greater display of love than for one to lay down himself for another. What could we lay down for our disciples? Our insecurities, our pride, our treasures, our time, and so on. In reference to making disciples, we could say, "Greater love has no one than this, that someone lay aside themselves for a time to pour into another all that they are." Love must be the driving force behind every word we speak and everything that we do.

Proper Discipleship

We now understand how we are supposed to operate in the process of making disciples (know them, know Him personally, walk by faith and not by sight, operate in humility, and do all in love). The question then becomes, what does it truly mean to make a disciple, and what does a disciple look like?

Jesus said, "You are the light of the world. A city set on a hill cannot be hidden. Nor do people light a lamp and put it under a basket, but on a stand, and it gives light to all in the house. In the same way, let your light shine before others, so that they may see your good works and give glory to your Father who is in heaven" (Matthew 5:14-16). Often when disciples are talked about, this is what our minds go to, those whom our lights shine onto. However, such is not the case. Paul stated, "for at one time you were darkness, but now you are light in the Lord. Walk as children of light (for the fruit of light is found in all that is good and right and true)" (Ephesians 5:8-9). Also, John declared, "in him was life, and the life was the light of men" (John 1:4). The Light that shines forth through us has nothing to do with us, it is simply His life that made us alive and is now being shown through us. Meaning, the Light that others see simply comes from being made alive in Him, and if others do not see His Light in you, then you need to examine the state of your life, literally. This is important to understand. For since He was the Light manifested, that means He was always shining forth the Light. Understanding this we are brought to an important question: Since His Light was constantly shining, did everyone He come in contact with become His disciple? The simple answer is no.

This is crucial for us to understand. For we are directly commissioned by Him to make disciples. If we think that by simply walking in His Light that we are making disciples, we are wrong. We have to restructure how we think about discipleship. Many of us think that everyone we interact with, everyone we work with, and everyone we are close to are our disciples because, again, our definition of discipleship is simply, anyone onto whom the Light of Jesus shines. We think that making disciples is easy, something that can be done with little to no effort, but this is incorrect. Let's look to our example, Jesus. This is what the Gospel of Luke tells us: "In these days he went out to the mountain to pray, and all night he continued in prayer to God. And when day came, he called his disciples and chose from them twelve, whom he named apostles" (Luke 6:12-13). This is what we see: before Jesus went out to find His disciples, He first prayed. Furthermore, He didn't pray a small, five-minute prayer. Luke states that "all night he continued in prayer." Meaning, His prayer was one of fervency. It was a prayer of intentionality. It was a prayer of passion. Why? Why did he pray so passionately over whom would become His disciples?

The answer to these questions comes from a proper understanding of what a disciple is. "Disciples" from Luke

Kingdom Progression

6 is "mathētēs," and it means "a learner or a pupil." This simple understanding falls short of the true scope of this word. In his commentary on this chapter, David Guzik states, "A disciple was a learner, a student, but in the first century a student did not simply study a subject; he followed a teacher. There was an element of personal attachment in 'disciple' that is lacking in 'student.'" We think that if we casually talk about Jesus to someone, they automatically become our disciples. This is not the case. This may very well be the birth of a new disciple, but they are not yet your disciple. This is key to remember. There has to be a starting point, but that starting point cannot also be the end of the matter. It may start with casual conversation, but unless it grows into something more, a disciple is not born. Look to when He called His disciples. He said to them, "Follow me, and I will make you fishers of men" (Matthew 4:19). Casual conversation was not the point in which they became His disciples; it was when they began to follow Him. They went where He went, listened intently to all that He said, and watched with purpose all that He did. Then the point in time came when they began to do all that He had done and say what He said. This would have never come about unless they first followed and became His disciples.

Why do you think that at His trial the people in the crowd kept pointing out that Peter was with Jesus? Because he had truly been His disciple and had so become like Him that they could see Him on Peter (see Luke 22:54-62). This is the key to understanding what a disciple is. They were His legacy. After His resurrection, when He was no longer actively working on the earth in His physical body, it was the disciples that would become His voice, it was the disciples that would become His hands, and it was the disciples that would become His feet. This is why He agonized all night in prayer over who He would choose. Because whomever He chose would become the image of Him to the next generation. After His resurrection, when a new generation would arise that never knew Jesus during His earthly ministry, His disciples would be the only ones who would be able to convey Him to them. This is why He agonized over this.

Paul embodied this thought beautifully: "Be imitators of me, as I am of Christ" (I Corinthians 11:1). Paul passionately sought after becoming more and more and more like Christ. However, he didn't stop there. He called out to those who claimed to believe: "Become my disciples by intentionally doing what I do, saying what I say, and going where I go, just as I do so to Christ." This is the proper understanding of what a disciple is, one who intentionally pursues after another to become like them. It is intentional and purposeful. There is no such thing as "they don't know that they're your disciple." Being a disciple means recognizing that another has something that you don't, and so, desiring to attain what they have, you will do anything to attain such.

Additionally, the strain of discipleship does not stop there, for Paul said, "Bear one another's burdens, and so fulfill the law of Christ" (Galatians 6:2). In reference to discipleship, this is what this means: when they first come to the truth, they are going to have no foundation. It's not just that their foundation isn't going to be strong, it's that in the beginning, it won't even exist. If they have no foundation, what are they going to stand on? Your foundation, or in other words, you. They are going to be standing on your shoulders as you carry them until they can stand on their own. This is not going to happen overnight; you may have to bear the weight of them for months or years. This bearing is crucial, for if we don't carry them on our shoulders, and pick them up with our hands, they will not make it. They need us. Many might hear this and try to avoid discipleship, for it sounds too difficult. There's too much work involved, and so on. Yes, discipleship is hard, and yes, it's not easy, but this does not excuse us from it. I remember several years ago Brother Stan Gleason came to the church I attend and

Kingdom Progression

spoke on discipleship. He defined such as "the cross which you carry." I have never forgotten that, but I fear many of us have (or never knew it to begin with). Discipleship is a heavy burden, but it is a burden we are called to bear.

Again, we think that everyone around us is our disciple. No, everyone around you (hopefully) sees His Light, but if they are not intentionally following you as you pour into them, they are not yet your disciple. This is the biblical definition of what it is to be a disciple.

Another thing that we do not understand is that we think we should continually pour into an individual again, and again, and again, even though they have rejected His Light and truth and hope every single time. This is not the biblical way.

"And he said to them, 'The harvest is plentiful, but the laborers are few. Therefore pray earnestly to the Lord of the harvest to send out laborers into his harvest. Go your way; behold, I am sending you out as lambs in the midst of wolves. Carry no moneybag, no knapsack, no sandals, and greet no one on the road. Whatever house you enter, first say, Peace be to this house!' And if a son of peace is there, your peace will rest upon him. But if not, it will return to you. And remain in the same house, eating and drinking what they provide, for the laborer deserves his wages. Do not go from house to house. Whenever you enter a town and they receive you, eat what is set before you. Heal the sick in it and say to them, The kingdom of God has come near to you.' But whenever you enter a town and they do not receive you, go into its streets and say, Even the dust of your town that clings to our feet we wipe off against you. Nevertheless know this, that the kingdom of God has come near.' I tell you, it will be more bearable on that day for Sodom than for that town'" (Luke 10:2-12). This is the truth of the matter: time is too short for us to be wasting time on people that don't want it. That sounds harsh, but it is the truth. If Jesus admonished His disciples to keep moving on, how much more urgency ought we to have to find those who truly want it, with His return coming ever so quickly?

Paul displayed this mindset time and time again. We read multiple times throughout the Book of Acts, how he would go to a new city and go first to the synagogue. However, when the Jews rejected the truth, he did not continue with them or beg them to understand. No, it says, "And Paul and Barnabas spoke out boldly, saying, 'It was necessary that the word of God be spoken first to you. Since you thrust it aside and judge yourselves unworthy of eternal life, behold, we are turning to the Gentiles'" (Acts 13:46). A few verses later it says, "And the word of the Lord was spreading throughout the whole region. But the Jews incited the devout women of high standing and the leading men of the city, stirred up persecution against Paul and Barnabas, and drove them out of their district. But they shook off the dust from their feet against them and went to Iconium. And the disciples were filled with joy and with the Holy Spirit" (Acts 13:49-52). They conveyed the exact response admonished by Jesus for us to have.

Do not twist this. This cannot be our excuse to never make disciples. If we just constantly say, "Well, they weren't meant to be my disciple," and simply say that time and time again as an "out," then we forsake the most fundamental call on our lives, "go therefore and make disciples…" No matter what your specific calling or office or position, this commission dwells at the heart of it all. If we forsake this, we forsake all. Jesus said, "Not everyone who says to me, 'Lord, Lord,' will enter the kingdom of heaven, but the one who does the will of my Father who is in heaven. On that day many will say to me, 'Lord, Lord, did we not prophesy in your name, and cast out demons in your name, and do many mighty works in your name?' And then will I declare to them, 'I never knew you; depart from me, you workers of lawlessness'" (Matthew 7:21-23). What is His will that we must do? (Matthew 28:19-20) Once again, we have to

Kingdom Progression

properly understand what it means to be a disciple if we are ever going to make them disciples.

We must have balance, though. For Jesus gave a critical parable in the Gospel of Luke that must be taken into account wherein discipleship is discussed.

> And he told this parable: "A man had a fig tree planted in his vineyard, and he came seeking fruit on it and found none. And he said to the vinedresser, 'Look, for three years now I have come seeking fruit on this fig tree, and I find none. Cut it down. Why should it use up the ground?' And he answered him, 'Sir, let it alone this year also, until I dig around it and put on manure. Then if it should bear fruit next year, well and good; but if not, you can cut it down.'"
> -Luke 13:6-9

The nature of the fig tree must be examined before this parable can be fully understood. This was taken from an article by Jonathan Madore on growing fig trees: "A tree will bear fruit 3 to 4 years after planting, but this can vary a bit depending on variety and environmental conditions." Taking this information back to the parable, we see that the tree was in its third-year post-planting. This is why the vinedresser advised the master of the crop to wait one more year, because to cut it down then would be to cut it down prematurely. The fig tree still had the potential to bear fruit.

When the seed (which is the Word of God [see Luke 8:11]) has been planted in the soil (which is the heart [see Luke 8:15]), we cannot expect a harvest immediately. We must be patient and give it space in which to grow. Additionally, not every fig tree will bear fruit in the same period of time. Some bear at the beginning of that three-year mark, others edge at the end of the four years. We cannot come to discipleship expecting to see the same thing every time. We will quickly become discouraged this way and prematurely cut down our disciples before giving them a chance to bear fruit. We must remember that each disciple is unique; therefore, this is why we began this chapter by examining the importance of knowing the individual personally. Due to each individual being unique, each walk will be unique. This is why we cannot hold an exact standard for how it ought to look every time.

  Again, we must have proper balance. We cannot simply operate in the mentality of constantly moving on to the next tree (person), but we also cannot wait for a tree that may never bear fruit, just as the vinedresser said, cut it down after the fourth year. There must be harmony. This requires discernment. Is the person receiving the truth you are speaking to them at all? Or are they shutting you out and ignoring you? If they don't want it, you have to find those that do. However, if they are listening to your words and soaking up the truth that you are presenting to them, don't cut them down. Properly care for the tree that you planted; water it, and give it space and time to grow. There has to be harmony between these two principles, for to lean too far to either side is to hinder growth. For if we are always moving, we will never plant. On the other hand, if we are never moving, we will never reap a harvest. We have to know when to move, and when to wait.

  We have a world to reach, this is why proper discipleship is so important. Discipleship, as mentioned when speaking about Jesus' disciples, is our legacy. It is through disciples that the truth that we live and die by is passed on to generations long after we are gone. If we never make a true disciple, who is going to pass it on? This is why we must be led by prayer. Prayer is the key. We must be prayerfully led by Him to those who truly desire truth. We cannot spend all our time and energy pouring into someone who does not want it; we will never reach our world this

Kingdom Progression

way. The only way we will reach our world is by following His pattern. Prayerful discipleship.

Interwoven with discipleship is the spiritual principle of multiplication. What does this mean? Let's say a new discipleship generation begins with me. I go and disciple three people according to the biblical definition thereof. Then they go and do the same. That three immediately becomes nine. Then those nine go and do the same. That nine becomes twenty-seven. Those twenty-seven do the same and it becomes eighty-one. Across those four discipleship generations, one hundred and twenty people were reached. This is how we are going to reach our world and ensure that there is a Church for the generations to come, by obeying and following His example of true discipleship.

Conclusion

As already stated, discipleship lies at the core of all that we do, no matter what position or title we hold. If we are not making disciples, we have then abandoned the will of God. The issue is that not all are intentionally ignoring His commission; many are ignorantly doing so, thinking that they are indeed making disciples when all they are truly doing is being a light. Do not misunderstand, this is important too, for it is His Light that oftentimes initially draws people to you. However, this cannot be our crutch, for many saw the Light of Jesus and never followed. We must be intentional and seek those who desire and hunger for truth and righteousness.

Understanding the proper structure of discipleship is critical to the continuing of His Church; it is what He implemented to ensure His Church would last for thousands of generations. If we abandon such, or do it incorrectly, we run the serious risk of dying off. We must understand discipleship and pursue it purposefully.

Epilogue

My mind goes to a conversation I had with one whom my wife and I teach a Bible Study. We were talking about the Bible and knowing the Bible and how vast and far-reaching and how deep the Bible is. Due to this conversation, he asked me, "Should I not tell people that I know the Bible then?" I paused for a moment, for no one had ever asked me a question like that before. My answer was this: "If you think about it, to claim that one knows the Bible is truly a very arrogant thought, for God is His Word and God is infinite, meaning, His Word is infinite. Considering such, how could one truly 'know' His Word? Rather, I think that we ought to more rightly say that we are 'students of His Word.'"

Here at the close of this book, this is simply what I want to encourage you all to do and be: be forever students of the Word of God. Never grow stale or cold or dry. Never become complacent or slothful. Grab hold once again of that zeal you once had. Light the fire of passion for His Word inside your heart once more. It is easy to reach a point where you think you understand all there is to understand about a particular subject. You've studied it. Read books about it. Studied it some more. Now you have a good understanding of it to where you can confidently talk about that subject with someone with no sort of reference notes at all. That is fantastic, but don't stop there. I guarantee you that there is still more that you don't know. Study again. Read the books again and find other books on the topic. Then study again and again and again. Remember though, we do not study to attain good sermon notes, we study so that we might know Him in a greater way.

I quoted this Scripture earlier, but it bears repeating: "But grow in the grace and knowledge of our Lord and Savior Jesus Christ. To him be the glory both now and to the day of eternity. Amen" (II Peter 3:18). No matter where you find yourself in this particular moment, whether it's sitting in a pew, waiting for God to show you your place in all this, or behind the pulpit, I admonish you to grow. Keep growing. There's always more.

Some may be discouraged by that line of thought: there's always more. Don't be discouraged; be encouraged. For how boring would it be if we served a God who could be fully and completely understood by our finite brains? Would that also not be concerning? If you could understand all that He is, that would imply that all that He is, is not that great. This would imply that you serve a puny god. Thankfully, you don't. There is more to Him than our minds can perceive. We can reach for all eternity and forever find more to grab hold of. This ought to be the most exciting thought we've ever had. This affirms to us that our God is great, and greatly to be praised. His riches are untold. His grace, limitless. His mercy, new every morning. He really is a great God.

Repeating what was said in the introduction, we must understand the technicalities of His Kingdom and ministry, but it is much more important to understand the heart of God behind it all. While you pursue greater understanding, even more so pursue a greater relationship, both with Him and those around you. Knowing the technicalities of the Gifts of the Spirit means nothing without love driving such, as Paul said in I Corinthians 13:1-3. Paul also said, "Let all that you do be done in love" (I Corinthians 16:14).

Jesus has a place for every one of us in the Body. We all play a crucial part, and even one part missing or out of order throws off the rest. We hear that all the time and think it's just rhetoric preachers use to get people to engage, such could not be further from the truth. You are vital, and no one can replace you. I need you just as much as you need me. Therefore, one final time I admonish you to diligently pursue Him and grow.

Kingdom Progression

Book Recommendations

To further aid in continued growth, below I have listed several books that I have read over the years that have aided me in my personal growth. I pray that they bless you as they blessed me.

~The New Birth by David Bernard
~In Search of Holiness by David Bernard
~Practical Holiness: A Second Look by David Bernard
~Spiritual Disciplines for the Christian Life by Donald S. Whitney
~Spiritual Disciplines: Essential Practices of the Christian Life by various authors (edited by Robin Johnson and Karen Myers)
~The Unflawed Leader by Stan Gleason
~7 Levels of Spiritual Maturity by Anita Joy Sargeant
~Spiritual Leadership: In The Twenty-First Century by David Bernard
~Spiritual Gifts by David Bernard
~Gifts of the Spirit by Lee Stoneking
~The Five-Fold Ministry and Spiritual Gifts: An Apostolic Pattern by Douglas Klinedinst
~The Five-Fold Ministry and Spiritual Insights by Lee Stoneking
~Fivefold Ministry by I.R. Womack
~Doctrines of the Bible by various authors (edited by J.L. Hall and David Bernard)
~Follow to Lead by Stan Gleason
~Discipled Together by Brandon Cremean

Above all else, the Word of God. No book could ever compare to what the Word of God has to say. No words penned by any author could ever replace personal study done

Kristopher David Grepke

by the individual. Read books, yes, they are a magnificent resource that ought to be used. Leaders are readers. Even more so, get in His Word.

With all love in Jesus Christ,
Kristopher David Grepke

www.ingramcontent.com/pod-product-compliance
Lightning Source LLC
Chambersburg PA
CBHW060517100426
42743CB00009B/1356